Library of
Davidson College

# Taxation of Multinationals in Communist Countries

# Paul Jonas

The Praeger Special Studies program, through a selective worldwide distribution network, makes available to the academic, government, and business communities significant and timely research in U.S. and international economic, social, and political issues.

# Taxation of Multinationals in Communist Countries

PRAEGER SPECIAL STUDIES IN INTERNATIONAL BUSINESS, FINANCE, AND TRADE

**Praeger Publishers**   New York   London

Library of Congress Cataloging in Publication Data

Jonas, Paul, 1922-
    Taxation of multinationals in communist countries.

    (Praeger special studies in international business, finance, and trade)
    Includes bibliographical references.
    1. International business enterprises—Taxation—Communist countries.  I. Title.
HD2755.5.J66    1978    336.2'43'091717    77-13886
ISBN 0-03-040676-5

PRAEGER SPECIAL STUDIES
200 Park Avenue, New York, N.Y., 10017, U.S.A.

Published in the United States of America in 1978
by Praeger Publishers,
A Division of Holt, Rinehart and Winston, CBS, Inc.

89    038    987654321

© 1978 by Praeger Publishers

*All rights reserved*

Printed in the United States of America

# PREFACE AND ACKNOWLEDGMENTS

An extensive program of desk research on the legal aspects, trade regulations, business customs, and fiscal rules of the selected European socialist countries of Yugoslavia, Romania, Hungary, Bulgaria, and Czechoslovakia started this project. In this first phase, relevant sections of various yearbooks, bulletins, publications of central statistical offices, catalogues of trade fairs, and journals on the countries published both within and outside the Soviet bloc were examined.

This first phase was followed by primary or field research carried out in the selected countries. Such research was vital to obtaining a total and precise picture of fiscal regulations affecting Western corporations. It should be noted here that tax decrees are often not applicable or not applied in practice but are substituted for by various financial statutory rules. An extensive program was conducted including interviews with government officials, managerial personnel, and academics. In addition, several unpublished documents were collected, showing how Western firms, operating with Eastern socialist enterprises with limited equity participation, are being taxed.

Important collaboration was received from the U.S. embassies in the respective countries. Thanks should be expressed to Helen C. Batjer, deputy chief of mission, Joseph Elson Lee, first secretary, and Eric Edward Svenson, second secretary, in Sofia; Henry A. Clarke, commercial attaché, in Bucharest; Charles Thomas York, counselor for economic and commercial affairs, William J. Waller, commercial attaché, Leopold Gotzlinger, first secretary, in Belgrade; Robert W. Farrand, chief, Economic/Commercial Section, in Prague. They were all most helpful with information and arranging contacts and meetings.

Local government officials were equally helpful in furnishing additional information and clarifying questions. Tzvetan Kavdanski, chief of INTERPRED, George Manolov, director of Vitocha, in Sofia; Marin Vidroiu, chief of double taxation, Tempe Ion, chief of tax revenues, Melchiade A. Popp, councilor from the Ministry of Finance, George Cojocaru, Canadian Desk Offices and Dumitru Ionescu, councilor, both in the Ministry of Foreign Trade, in Bucharest; Bozedar Braovich, assistant secretary of finance, Miodrag Arsic, councilor, Office of Taxation, Ministry of Finance, in Belgrade gave the author many much needed insights.

Among the academics, N. M. Todorov, director, Institut d'Etudes Balkaniques; Maria Kisenliceva, professor of history, in Sofia; N. Fotino, director, l'Association de Droit International et de Relations Internationales de la R.S. de Roumanie; Vlad Georgescu, Institut de Studii Sudest Europene; Silvin Bruncan, former ambassador to the United States, in Bucharest; Miodrag

Sikujasovic, Institute of International Politics and Economics, in Belgrade; and Olga Kralova, professor of history in Prague, gave supplementary information.

István Deák, director, Institute on East Central Europe, Columbia University supplied background material and other helpful information.

Interviews were also conducted with business executives: Kenneth N. Yeager, assistant general manager, Rom Control Data Sr. 1 in Bucharest, and Milan Kovacevic, director, International Investment Corporation for Yugoslavia, in Belgrade gave information as to the practicalities of joint ventures and their taxation.

In Austria, invaluable information on tax treaties and other aspects of international fiscal regulations was received from Helmut Berger, Budesministerum für Finanzen, Vienna.

Several visits to the Vienna Institute for Comparative Economic Studies also resulted in tangible help. Friedrick Levcik, director of research, and staff members Benedict Askanas, J. Stankovski, Carl H. McMillan, and David St. Charles (the last two originally from the East-West Project Institute of Soviet and East European Studies at Carleton University (Ottawa) gave a warm reception and valuable information.

The U.S. Department of Commerce East-West Center in Vienna opened its files on taxation on Western enterprise; S. Douglas Martin, director of the center, and Willy K. Kosek, commercial adviser, were most helpful in discussing various issues related to the project.

Radio Free Europe in Munich furnished valuable information in the form of research materials and allowed the author to listen to the monitoring of the radio stations of the selected European socialist countries on the issue of cooperation with Western enterprises. Ralph Walter, director, James Brown, head of research, and Harry Trend, head of economic research, are to be thanked for increasing considerably the primary sources used for this study.

The field research was concluded by a round-table conference at the U.S. Department of Treasury, where the author benefited from the remarks of members of the International Tax Staff and other treasury and U.S. government representatives.

János Horváth, Distinguished Professor of Economics at Butler University, acted as a consultant for the project and visited Hungary for the missing link. He came back with considerable material on taxation of Western enterprise in Hungary, which he obtained from government officials, managers of joint corporations, and academics.

The third phase of the project was to digest the material, and, since one cannot shed one's skin, to provide a theoretical framework dealing with the taxation of Soviet-type economies. In Albuquerque, my graduate assistant, John Hof, helped with the tedious work of selecting out the important material from the bulky collected papers that filled up several suitcases; he also produced the graphs.

Last but not least, I am grateful to the Office of Tax Analysis, U.S. Department of Treasury, for enabling me to undertake this "joint venture" with the abovementioned collaborators and to Gary C. Hufbauer, Deputy Assistant Secretary of the Treasury for his patience, help, and encouragement. The views expressed, the errors and inadequacies are, of course, the responsibility of the author.

Albuquerque, New Mexico<br>
May 1977

# CONTENTS

|  | Page |
|---|---|
| PREFACE AND ACKNOWLEDGMENTS | v |
| LIST OF TABLES AND FIGURES | x |

Chapter

### 1 INTRODUCTION — 1

Notes — 4

### 2 THEORETICAL APPROACHES TO COMMUNIST TAXATION — 5

A Model of Soviet-Type Taxation — 5
Conclusion — 9
A Model for Estimating Economic Growth Potential — 10
Notes — 13

### 3 THE JOINT VENTURE — 14

The Concept of the Joint Venture — 14
  Forms of the Joint Business Venture — 15
  Characteristics of Joint Business Ventures in Various Locations — 16
Case Studies of Joint Ventures — 17
  Yugoslavia — 18
  Romania — 20
  Hungary — 21
  COMECON — 22
Notes — 24

### 4 TAXATION OF THE FOREIGN SHARE IN COMMUNIST COUNTRIES — 25

Yugoslavia — 25
  The Market-Socialist System — 25
  Ownership — 26
  Restrictions on Foreign Investments — 28
  Taxation of Joint Ventures — 29
  Taxation of Citizens and Foreign Nationals — 34
Romania — 40
  A Strict Centrally Planned System — 40
  Ownership — 41

|   |   |
|---|---|
| Taxation of Joint Ventures | 42 |
| The Effects of Tax on the Foreign Investor: An Economic Analysis | 45 |
| Taxation of Nonresident and Foreign Nationals | 50 |
| A Summary of the Romanian Taxation System | 51 |
| Hungary | 52 |
| A Liberal and Open Centrally Planned System | 52 |
| Ownership | 53 |
| Taxation of Joint Ventures | 54 |
| Taxation of Foreign Employees | 59 |
| Summary of the Financial Operation of Joint Ventures in Hungary | 62 |
| Bulgaria | 63 |
| Stressing Economic Cooperation with the Soviet Union | 63 |
| Regulations on Foreign Economic Cooperation | 64 |
| Personal Income Tax Rates and Tax on Profits of Corporations | 65 |
| The Bulgarian Joint Venture | 67 |
| A Bulgarian Representative of Foreign Firms: INTERPRED | 68 |
| A Summary of the Operations of Joint Ventures and Their Taxation in Bulgaria | 69 |
| Czechoslovakia | 69 |
| Czechoslovakia: "Classic" Soviet-Type Model | 69 |
| Regulations on Foreign Economic Cooperation | 70 |
| The System of Taxation in Czechoslovakia | 71 |
| Summary of Western Cooperation with Czechoslovakia | 72 |
| Notes | 73 |
| **5 CONCLUSIONS AND POSTSCRIPT** | **74** |
| Conclusions | 74 |
| Postscript | 78 |
| **APPENDIX: A LIST OF YUGOSLAV STATUTES OF RELEVANCE TO FOREIGN INVESTMENT** | **82** |
| **BIBLIOGRAPHY** | **86** |
| **ABOUT THE AUTHOR** | **89** |

## LIST OF TABLES AND FIGURES

| Table | | Page |
|---|---|---|
| 2.1 | Data of Snowflake Diagrams | 12 |
| 4.1 | Yugoslav Joint Ventures by Foreign Partner's Country and Contribution as of January 7, 1973 | 29 |
| 4.2 | Geographical Distribution of Foreign Invested Capital Within Yugoslavia as of January 7, 1973 | 30 |
| 4.3 | Nontaxable Amount, 1973 | 36 |
| 4.4 | Minimum and Maximum Base Tax Rates | 38 |
| 4.5 | Tax Burden, for Two-to-Four-Member Families | 38 |
| 4.6 | 1966 and 1973 Tax Rates | 66 |
| 5.1 | Corporate Income Tax Rates of Western Countries | 79 |

| Figure | | |
|---|---|---|
| 2.1 | Model of Internal Price Distortion cum Hidden Income Taxation | 7 |
| 2.2 | Snowflake Diagrams | 11 |

# Taxation of Multinationals in Communist Countries

# CHAPTER 1

# INTRODUCTION

The literature dealing with economic relations with the East European countries and with international fiscal measures affecting these relationships is motley. It has an extremely wide range and includes specialist-oriented scholarly analytical studies and emotionally charged newspaper and magazine articles. The subject has lately been supplemented by a seemingly new topic —the question and problems of joint ventures with East European countries. Writers in this topic reveal the *goût de canaille,* the commoner's taste, and approach the question with a descriptive treatment of published texts, their aim being to provide a compendium for practitioners.

The aim of this study is to strike a balance between the theoretical and the pragmatic. The study argues that the phenomenon of joint ventures with East European countries and related aspects of fiscal regulation are not new. Investments of Western firms in Eastern Europe were commonplace before and shortly after World War II when these countries were not organized under centrally planned frameworks. Even the Soviet Union provides examples in her own history that restrictive economic division at the Elbe is not an iron rule and does not conflict with Marxist-Leninist theory.

In one of its most colorful zigzags, Soviet commercial policy is now back to the spirit of the early phase of the Revolution. On a wintry day late in 1920, a decree signed by V. Ulianov (Lenin) was published in Moscow. The startled world learned from this resolution that the Russian Soviet Socialist Republic was appealing to the more highly developed industrial countries for technical and material assistance in restoring the Russian productive forces that had been depleted by World War I. The decree listed in six paragraphs the rights and guarantees that would be extended to concessionaries.[1]

V. I. Lenin always argued for a policy of peaceful coexistence with countries that had different social systems and for maximum utilization of international cooperation and division of labor. "The most urgent, vital, practical, and acutely revealed interests of all capitalist powers in recent years," said Lenin in 1922, "demand the development, regularization, and expansion of trade with Russia. And since these interests exist, one may argue, one may quarrel, one may differ on various combinations—it is even very likely that there will be reasons to differ—but, nonetheless, ultimately this basic economic necessity will pave its own way."[2] In 1921-25, Soviet Russia concluded over 40 trade agreements and treaties with over 20 countries.

In the late 1920s and early 1930s, the Soviet Union established agreements on delivery of equipment, acquisition of licenses, and technical assistance with such large firms as Ford Motor Company, General Electric, Westinghouse Electric, United States Steel, and Du Pont de Nemours.[3] In 1931, for example, 40 percent of total American exports of machinery and equipment went to the Soviet Union.[4] In the West, commercial interest, profit, and striving to penetrate a new market proved stronger than political hostility and ideological enmity toward the Soviet system.

At the end of the 1930s, the champions of self-styled isolationism took over in Russia, claiming that it was impossible for the Soviet Union to maintain normal peaceful relations with her capitalist encirclement, and a policy of maximum economic self-sufficiency was established. This trend was helped by the approach of World War II; Stalin with his circle argued that the Western world would use the opportunity to withhold delivery of certain vitally important types of products from the Soviet states in order to push it toward its downfall.

During the war years, however, a broad collaboration developed among the allied powers. J. Davies, former U.S. ambassador to Moscow, emphasized that aid to the Soviet Union was dictated first and foremost by U.S. national interest, since "Russian resistance has become a matter of life and death for all of us."[5]

In 1946, the cold war was launched, and the United States and her West European allies adopted a policy aimed at the total curtailment of economic relations with communist countries. An economic blockade, however, is always a two-edged weapon; it is not clear who suffers the most from it—the blockaded or the blockaders.

In the 1960s, the majority of the Western countries and Japan took certain steps to reduce restrictions on imports from centrally planned economies and also gradually abandoned the strict practice of refusing to grant those countries credit in excess of five years. On the whole, Western Europe has adopted a long-range and comprehensive approach to the development of economic cooperation with the Soviet Union and her East European allies.

During the last few years, after many decades of limbo, the governments of the United States and the Soviet Union have also been working toward agreements that aim to restore more normal commercial and business relationships between the two countries. Encouraging progress has been made, and this has been watched closely by the socialist European countries. The reason for their attentiveness is obvious: The economies of these smaller states can benefit even more than the Soviet economy from international economic cooperation with the United States. In short, the slogan, "commercial and trade issues move to the frontier," formulated by General Secretary Leonid Brezhnev, has become generally accepted throughout the Soviet bloc.

Quick, easy, and dramatic results are not expected, but in an era in which the cold war has given way to a policy of detente and peaceful coexistence, the lure of mutual benefits creates a pressure for establishment of joint business ventures.

While the potential benefits of increased business relations between the Western and Soviet bloc countries are clear, there remain, nonetheless, a number of difficult issues that will require resolution before the benefits can be realized, and many complex questions need to be answered.[6]

In this project we have selected a single issue within this given situation and will attempt to answer the question, "What are the fiscal rules in selected European socialist countries that apply to foreign corporations?"

A basic rule of international fiscal law suggests that a fair deal is being applied to foreign business ventures in host countries if the status of equality is observed—that is, if the tax burdens on the foreign ventures are the same as those on the domestic enterprises. This rule, however, cannot be applied to the foreign share of business establishments in centrally planned economies. In these countries, the state allocates the capital to the socialist firms; therefore, a liability arises to pay tax on assets and on the centralized portion of depreciation allowances. One can consider these types of taxes as interest payments. The foreign corporations that allocate capital from independent sources should, *ab ovo,* be exempted from these types of burdens. Similarly, these enterprises cannot expect either budget subsidies or governmental funds matching their losses.

What, then, are the guiding rules for determining taxation of Western enterprise in Eastern European systems? The following questions will be investigated for Yugoslavia, Romania, Hungary, Bulgaria, and Czechoslovakia:

The nature of limitations on the formation of foreign associations in key sectors such as banking, insurance, transportation, public services, and strategic raw material resources;

The types of business organizations (for example, corporate, partnership, branch office) in which foreigners may participate, and the definition of taxable income applied by the Eastern European countries in each case;

Types and rates of tax "normally" levied on corporate income and potential tax holidays;

Treatment of depreciation allowances;

Provision of investment credits and other capital subsidies;
Taxes on profit remittances, interest, and royalties to nonresidents; and
The extent to which export profits are preferentially taxed.

In addition, the present study provides a theoretical framework dealing with the broader concepts of trade relations between price-directed and centrally planned systems. It is hoped that the findings will deepen our knowledge of international fiscal economics and comparative systems and that a basis for policy decisions will be provided for those at the federal and enterprise levels who deal with the various apsects of commercial treaties and business decisions.

## NOTES

1. See, for a description of the decree and the performance of the early concessions, Joseph Wastein, "Soviet Economic Concessions: The Agony and the Promise," *Association for Comparative Economic Studies Bulletin* 16, 1 (Spring 1974).

2. V. I. Lenin, *Poln. sobr. soch.* (Collected Works, in Russian), vol. 45, p. 71.

3. *Sovetsko-amerikanskie otnosheniia*, 1919–1933 (Moscow, 1934), pp. 98–99.

4. S. Shmelev, "New Horizons of Economic Relations," *Mirovaia ekonomika i mezhdunarodnye otnosheniia*, no. 1, 1973.

5. J. Davies, *Mission to Moscow* (New York: and Harper and Row, 1943), p. 320.

6. Peter G. Peterson, *U.S.-Soviet Commercial Relationships in a New Era* (Washington, D.C.: Department of Commerce, August 1972), p. 3.

CHAPTER

# 2

## THEORETICAL APPROACHES TO COMMUNIST TAXATION

## A MODEL OF SOVIET-TYPE TAXATION

"Soviet taxation is a neglected field of study," remarked Franklyn Holzman in his 1955 book, *Soviet Taxation,*[1] and his complaint remains valid. Outside this book, no comprehensive work has been published by any Western author on the structure and working of Soviet-type fiscal measures. While many valuable studies touch on the peripheral and practical aspects of taxation as it exists in centrally planned economies, no theoretical attempt has been made, to our knowledge, to grasp the essentials or common characteristics of this type of taxation or to define its ideology.

The aim of this chapter, preceding the investigation of taxation of Western enterprise, is to provide a schematic representation of the main elements of the economic ideology affecting the collection of funds and the choice among different forms of taxation.

Taxation has an important role in the economic life of goal-oriented command systems in which a central planning board orders the composition of the product mix in such a way that the output of capital goods must always exceed replacement. To achieve this, a distorted price system is established that makes inputs cheap and consumption expensive. The tax system, therefore, is characterized by the dominance of excise taxes levied on consumer goods. This measure is based on the assumption that, among the population, especially in the agricultural sector, potential savings exceed actual savings. The population's unrevealed savings, therefore, should be the most important source of public capital accumulation.[2]

The nature of price distortions in a Soviet-type command economy stems from the rejection of the Bukharinist position in the famous "great industrialization debate," which argued that a market relationship between a free agricultural sector and a state-owned industrial sector could generate savings and investment in the former and could reduce costs and establish probability in the latter.[3]

Stalin accepted the leftist position that objected to an "agriculture-propelled economic development" and stressed speedy industrialization. The "super-industrializers" opposing N. I. Bukharin argued that capital accumulation should be squeezed out from the population and that the best method for this was an extreme excise tax system placed on consumer goods. Among the countries under discussion, this classical pattern is still relevant in Bulgaria, where corporate profit taxes do not exist and, therefore, prospective joint ventures, if Bulgarian authorities would agree to such associations, would not be taxed at all.

This position places little emphasis on technological innovation, which would improve marginal efficiency of capital in the respective sectors of the economy but regards growth simply as a direct function of investments allocated to the various categories of the productive processes with heavy emphasis in the capital goods sector.[4]

This continuous squeeze on the population, which uses an excise tax combined with the compulsory purchase of governmental bonds, can be illustrated easily.

In Figure 2.1, we assume that consumer goods subject to excise tax are on the x-axis and that everything else (capital goods purchased by households, savings) is on the y-axis and is measured in terms of money. The indifference curve map ($U_1 - U_4$) represents the tastes of the population. Let us also suppose that the households have take-home earnings of OT and that the budget line is TT'. With these assumptions, the point of equilibrium is at $P_1$ and the level of satisfaction is at $U_4$. An ad valorem excise tax on consumer goods will change the price opportunity line to something like AB. The population's equilibrium point is at $P_2$, and the utility level is slipped to $U_3$. The government, however, pocketed an amount TC of money as tax receipts. Now, let us suppose that the planner furnishes the market with only OJ amount of consumer goods. An equilibrium could be achieved by further increasing the rate of the excise tax and making the price of consumer goods even more expensive. Let us say that the planner's information indicates that this course means starvation for that part of the population in the lower income brackets.

The planner may feel that to starve part of the population will badly tarnish his country's international image; he thus selects another course. He will distribute the available OJ amount of consumer goods proportionately among the population at the taxed price ratio TB. The point of equilibrium, in this case, is on the budget line at point $P_3$ at the utility level $U_2$. $P_3$, however, clearly shows a disequilibrium. It indicates a serious inflationary gap; moreover, the governmental tax receipts have been reduced by an amount AC.

## FIGURE 2.1

Model of Internal Price Distortion cum Hidden Income Taxation

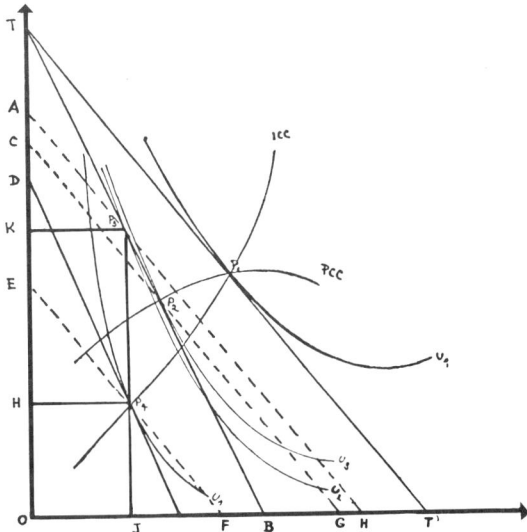

*Source:* Compiled by the author.

The planner will solve this problem by issuing governmental "peace" bonds for an amount TD and will make their purchase compulsory. Thus, the population's take-home pay is reduced to OD; with the taxed price ratio, the equilibrium point $P_4$ is achieved, which brings the level of satisfaction down to $U_1$. The amount TD can also be regarded as a hidden income tax, since a system is established whereby there is only a remote possibility that a government bond can be redeemed. This equilibrium wipes away the inflationary gap. The effect of "excise tax cum compulsory government bond" policy on the population is that the real income is reduced from OT to OE and the utility index from $U_4$ to $U_1$. The planner, however, is looking happily ahead. His capital accumulation is TD from the sales of government bonds and DE from excise taxes, a total amount of TE.

The movement between points $P_1$ and $P_4$ can be considered as successive income and substitution effects. ($P_1$ and $P_2$ lie on the same price consumption curve and $P_1$ and $P_4$ on the same income consumption or Engel curve.) The total change in the consumption mix can be explained, however, with a large income effect.

The planner, if the target utility function (something as $U_1$) and the planned quantity of consumer goods are given, can easily compute the magnitude of the excise tax and the amount of the governmental bonds to be sold to the population. When the results have been implemented, a static equilibrium occurs.

In the following arbitrary example, it will be proved that the planner can establish the exact rate of an ad valorem excise tax and the magnitude of an income tax (in the hidden form of compulsory purchase of government bonds) from his two targets: the selected consumer utility level and the planned amount of consumer goods. Thus

(1) $\overline{U} = q_1^a \ q_2^b$ ($\overline{U}$ is the level of satisfaction in the form of a utility index)

(2) $Y = p_1 \, q_1 + p_2 \, q_2$ (budget function)

The problem is a constraint minimum. The planner seeks to find the minimum real income (Y) by which the utility level (U) can be attained. The Lagrange multiplier method gives an easy solution.

$$Z = p_1 \, q_1 + p_2 \, q_2 + \lambda \, (\overline{U} - q_1^a \, q_2^b)$$

Taking the partials and equating to zero,

$$\frac{\partial Z}{\partial q_1} = p_1 - \lambda a q_1^{a-1} \, q_2^b = 0$$

$$\frac{\partial Z}{\partial q_2} = p_2 - \lambda b q_1^a \, q_2^{b-1} = 0$$

$$\frac{\partial Z}{\partial \lambda} = \overline{U} - q_1^a \, q_2^b = 0$$

Solving for $q_1$ and $q_2$,

(3) $q_1 = (\overline{U})^{\frac{1}{a+b}} \left(\dfrac{ap_2}{bp_1}\right)^{\frac{b}{a+b}}$

(4) $q_2 = (\overline{U})^{\frac{1}{a+b}} \left(\dfrac{bp_1}{ap_2}\right)^{\frac{a}{a+b}}$

From (3), if $q_1$, $p_2$, and $\overline{U}$ are known (in the graphical example in Figure 2.1 $q_1 = OJ$, $p_2 = 1$, and $\overline{U} = 1$), $p_1$ can be computed. Thus, the excise tax rate which should be levied on a starting price ratio can be established. (This initial price line in Figure 2.1 is TT'.)

When we know $p_1$ from (4), the amount of $q_2$ can be computed. Substituting back to the budget equation (2), we receive the minimum money income needed to attain the selected level of satisfaction, $\overline{U}$. (In Figure 2.1, this is $\overline{OD}$.) Thus, the amount of the hidden income tax is the difference between a starting income and the received minimum survival income (Figure 2.1, $\overline{OT} - \overline{OD} = \overline{TD}$.) As conditioning factors change, the concept of the minimum or survival income changes, too.

Static equilibrium is when coordination among the different production units assures a "good" correspondence with the effective aggregate demand. Dynamic equilibrium, on the other hand, may be defined as the achievement of a "satisfactory" growth rate and economic stability. It is said that price-directed economic systems are characterized by a dynamic disequilibrium and enjoy a static equilibrium whereas Soviet-type economic systems sacrifice static equilibrium in order to achieve a more valued dynamic equilibrium. The words "good" and "satisfactory" are relative, as are the terms equilibrium and disequilibrium.

Static or dynamic efficiency are not to be confused with equilibrium. We may define static efficiency as a situation when production conforms to the preferences of the community and when there is no possibility of increasing the production of one commodity without reducing the production of another. Dynamic efficiency can be measured by the hypothetical growth rate of the GNP with identical resource use and saving ratio.

## CONCLUSION

The basic feature of the centrally planned country's tax structure presented above, is the domination by an "excise tax cum compulsory governmental bond" system that aims to squeeze potential savings from the population by keeping the standard of living relatively low. It was also argued that Soviet-type policy in its "classical stage" concentrated heavily on increasing total investments and distributing these funds overwhelmingly in the capital goods sector, largely disregarding the (lowering) of capital-output ratios—that is, technological improvements.[5]

Taking into account the shortcomings of such a policy, the present trend in some of the command economies is to seek joint ventures in order to update their lagging technology and to learn new marketing methods in order to eliminate the chronic over- and underproduction so characteristic of a rigid centrally planned system.

In the present phase, when the governments of centrally planned economies face mounting pressure from their populations to increase per capita consumption, it is expected that commercial and other economic relations will respond to the existing political climate and, in an intertwined world, that the actual economic relations will equally influence the political mood of the countries involved. Economic relations in every form, therefore, seem to be a prerequisite to stablilizing the current lessening of political tensions and transforming confrontaton to competition.

## A MODEL FOR ESTIMATING ECONOMIC GROWTH POTENTIAL

The growth potential of the selected socialist countries of Yugoslavia, Romania, Hungary, Bulgaria, and Czechoslovakia can be important for Western enterprises aiming to establish joint ventures there. To demonstrate this point, we will use the so-called snowflake diagrams developed by the International Labour Organization.[6]

Snowflake diagrams demonstrate the distribution of employment across the major sectors of an economy and can be used for the analysis and prediction of growth potentials. The sectors selected are agriculture, manufacturing with mining, construction, transportation, commerce, and services. The diagrams are constructed on a six-axis graph with the percentage share of each sector plotted on one axis. Immature, developing economies are elongated upward along the agricultural axis. As the economy matures, the diagrams become more rounded, and, when the economy reaches the developed industrial stage, the snowflake "melts" as employment shifts heavily to the manufacturing and then to the services sectors.

It is proposed by the constructors of this model that in boom times an ample reserve of agriculturally employed labor is one of the basic ingredients of economic growth. This reserve initially provides low-cost, easily attracted labor and, later, a source for continued reinvestment (through savings and spendable income). The corollary of this proposition is, however, that the country should be ready to utilize current technological know-how, to link her economy to the international market, and to keep population growth controlled. The easiest way to achieve these prerequisites at least partially is to establish joint ventures with developed industrialized countries. Then, access to technology, secure capital formation, and knowledge of export and import markets are all more readily available.

The developed country, on the other hand, has a labor concentration in services and manufacturing rather than agriculture. A joint venture in a developing country would thus provide a fresh supply of underutilized labor and promote a similar growth effect in the developed country as well.

It is also pointed out that, because it freezes economic conditions, such cooperation can be risky and that joint ventures could more easily allow exploitation if the host country were more mature—that is, its snowflake more rounded.

Figure 2.2 gives the snowflake diagrams of the selected socialist countries. Table 2.1 gives corresponding numerical data. The following conclusions can be made from the material.

## FIGURE 2.2
## Snowflake Diagrams

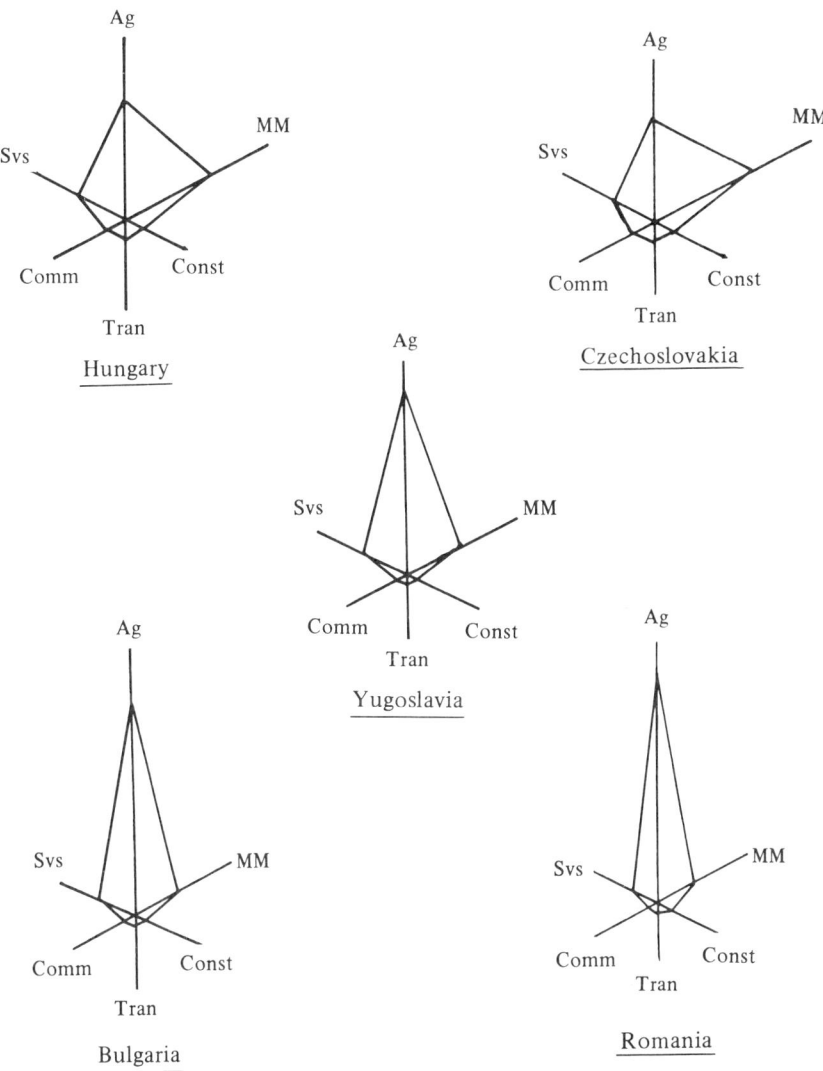

*Note:* Abbreviations used in this figure and in Table 2.1 are as follows: Ag—agriculture; MM—manufacturing with mining; Svs—services; Comm—commerce; Tran—transportation; Const—construction.

*Source: International Population Statistics Reports Series P-90* nos. 13, 14, 16, 18, 22, Bureau of the Census, U.S. Department of Commerce (Washington, D.C.: Government Printing Office, 1960–65).

All five countries have relatively high levels of agricultural employment. This sector can be characterized by disguised unemployment, underemployment, and relatively low incomes. Thus, by offering better opportunities, one could induce an exodus of the active and young agricultural labor force into attractive joint ventures. Western enterprise, therefore, can expect a readily available, relatively cheap labor force.

The countries that offer the largest labor pool are Bulgaria, Romania, and, to lesser degree, Yugoslavia. (In Yugoslavia, regional characteristics are especially important and will be discussed elsewhere.) Bulgaria is not ready at this time to be a host for joint ventures with Western enterprise, and her cooperation is limited for now to arrangements where other countries act as host. So, Romania and Yugoslavia, which actively seek foreign investment, especially as joint ventures, show the greatest potential for raw labor inputs. The labor here should be expected to be relatively untrained, and costs should be anticipated to upgrade the existing skills.

Hungary and Czechoslovakia show more concentration in their respective industrial sectors and services. Thus, the labor pool in these countries is composed of more sophisticated workers who will require higher wages and benefits, but lower training costs should be incurred.

On the basis of the snowflake diagrams, the following rule of thumb can be summarized for Western enterprises seeking joint ventures with the selected socialist countries:

### TABLE 2.1

Data of Snowflake Diagrams
(percent)

|  | Ag. | MM. | Svs. | Comm. | Tran. | Const. |
|---|---|---|---|---|---|---|
| Bulgaria | 64 | 16 | 11 | 3 | 3 | 3 |
| Romania | 70 | 13 | 8 | 3 | 2 | 4 |
| Czechoslovakia | 31 | 35 | 13 | 8 | 6 | 7 |
| Yugoslavia | 57 | 18 | 14 | 4 | 3 | 4 |
| Hungary | 36 | 30 | 16 | 7 | 6 | 5 |

*Note:* Figures are percentages of total work force employed in each sector.
*Source: International Population Statistics Reports Series P-90* nos. 13, 14, 16, 18, and 22; Bureau of the Census, U.S. Department of Commerce (Washington, D.C.: Government Printing Office, 1960–65).

In a production process characterized by a relatively low capital/labor ratio, Yugoslavia and Romania offer the best opportunities. (If regulations change, Bulgaria should be included here as well.) Further note should be made that Romania and Bulgaria are command economies giving full economic power to a central planning board, which orders the composition of the product mix in such a way that the output of capital goods must always exceed replacement and that a distorted price system makes inputs cheap and consumption expensive. In Yugoslavia, the framework is a more flexible market socialism where the decision-making power is in the hands of labor councils.

However, if the production is characterized by a relatively high capital/labor ratio, Hungary and Czechoslovakia should be preferred. (Czechoslovakia at present is not readily available for joint ventures with Western enterprises.) In these countries, a more educated labor force could provide a high degree of productivity when capital investments are adequate.

All these selected socialist countries have at least one common denominator: Their share of investment in GNP tends to be high. With the exception of Yugoslavia, they achieve this objective by keeping the goods earmarked for domestic consumption low and by curtailing the quantity of social services. Joint ventures, which bring capital investments, could ease this burden carried by the consumer. This is significant because Soviet-type systems are becoming more consumer oriented and are eager to reduce the social costs of speedy industrialization and economic growth.

## NOTES

1. Franklyn D. Holzman, *Soviet Taxation: The Fiscal and Monetary Problems of a Planned Economy* (Cambridge: Harvard University Press, 1955).
2. See Micha Gisser and Paul Jonas, "Soviet Growth in the Absence of Centralized Planning: A Hypothetical Alternative," *Journal of Political Economy* (March-April 1974).
3. See N. I. Bukharin, "Notes of an Economist at the Beginning of a New Economic Year." Reprinted in *Foundation of Soviet Strategy for Economic Growth: Selected Soviet Essays*, edited by Nicholas Spulber (Bloomington: Indiana University Press, 1964).
4. Evsey D. Domar, *Essays in the Theory of Economic Growth*, chapter 9, (New York: Oxford University Press, 1957); P. C. Mahalanobis, "Some Observations on the Process of Growth of National Income," *Sankyia: The Indian Journal of Statistics* 12 (September 1953).
5. Holzman, op. cit., and Robert T. Cole and Edward Maguire, "Tax Consequences of Transactions with the USSR," chapter in the American Bar Association Business Transaction with the Soviet Union (manuscript, June 8, 1974).
6. See, for a description, "Melting Snowflakes," *Economist* 253 (December 28, 1974):42.

CHAPTER

# 3

**THE JOINT VENTURE**

## THE CONCEPT OF THE JOINT VENTURE

Many people believe that the concept of the joint venture is something novel, a postwar concept created mainly to deal with developing countries, and that the national legislatures of the European socialist countries are not familiar enough with the different forms and combinations of the joint business venture to use it for their own benefit.[1] The following is a short compendium to describe the main features of the joint business venture and to contradict this belief.

The international joint venture has long been a familiar instrument of business association between enterprises of developed price-directed economies. Webster's International Dictionary defines this sort of business association as "a partnership of cooperative agreement between two or more partners, which is restricted to a single specific undertaking. Sometimes called also joint undertaking or joint venture."

This concept, even from the standpoint of the European socialist countries, should not be new. Joint ventures have been practiced by these countries. As a matter of fact, such associations have been created between socialist and developing countries. Some socialist enterprises also act as investors in joint undertakings in "fraternal" socialist countries. These facts negate the often heard allegation that one of the reasons for the hesitancy of some centrally planned economies to enter into this type of business association is that the legal framework for joint ventures has yet to be defined. Political considerations are most probably responsible for the reluctance.

The joint venture, as often stated, reconciles two interests. The foreign investor aims for the most effective protection for its property; moreover, it desires to enter a new market, to reach third markets through a new base, and to transfer production to a place where the costs of construction, labor, and so on, are lower than in his own country.

From the standpoint of the capital-importing host country, it is expected that the Western investor will furnish both tangibles and intangibles. Tangibles cover cash, machinery, raw materials, and intermediate goods; their value is easily established. Concerning intangibles, such as property rights (patents, trade marks, know-how, secret process techniques), good will, services, and assistance, it is more difficult to determine value, and the attitudes of the European socialist countries vary as regards these intangibles. In Romania, for example, "industrial property rights and other rights" may constitute payment for capital shares. But in other countries, know-how and secret processes may not be capitalized unless "represented by specific patents . . . or specific formulae of economic value."[2]

To sum up, the joint venture is a business association of comparatively long duration set up by two or more parties in order to run an enterprise subject to sharing of control, risk, and profit.

## Forms of the Joint Business Venture

Initial qualification of the joint business venture is on the basis of two criteria, namely, the nationality of the parties and the number of the parties. A distinction should be made between national and international joint ventures. The application of the second criterion gives the following variations: bilateral, tripartite, and multipartite ventures. When multipartite ventures are used among several partners belonging to different countries, we have the well-known multinational corporation.

The nature of the ownership of assets is a further qualification. Assets can be owned by private parties or by governmental agencies. In the West, joint ventures are most frequently concluded by private parties. However, it occurs fairly often that national or international ventures are established between a public agency and one or more private investors. In the case of the European socialist countries, publicly owned firms enter an agreement with private business associations.

Additional description can be constructed in accordance with the financing aspects of the joint business venture. In the most usual case, the capital, which includes the tangible and intangible assets of the association, is provided by a ratio or ratios determined by the contract. The partners may acquire their share from existing funds or from private lending institutions. They may also utilize a consortium of private firms. In the case of joint ventures with the European socialist countries, the host country's public national financial institutions stand behind the socialist firm to provide the equity determined in the contract.

The form of business association can also be used to define a joint business venture more precisely. The joint venture can be an incorporated or an unincorporated company.

A further qualification is the form of financing, namely, equity or nonequity. An equity business association is a corporation in which the equity is owned by the members who regard the enterprise as a separate entity and share the profits and the risks. A nonequity joint venture is a flexible personal association for noncontinuous business without any form of corporate body such as board of directors or general assembly of shareholders. It seeks a profit that is immediately divided. As a rule, a corporation is the sponsor of the project and has sole responsibility to third parties. Once the project is executed, the sponsor is reimbursed for his share of expenses. Thus, the constituent elements of an equity joint venture are body corporate, separate enterprise, and rights based on respective shares, while the rights of the partners in a nonequity contractual venture will be whatever is agreed in the contract.

## Characteristics of Joint Business Ventures in Various Locations

As mentioned above, the joint business venture, in its equity or nonequity form, between or among private investors, has been a commonplace in the price-directed industrial countries. One should mention, however, that major investors from the United States avoid entering an international joint venture or, often, even an industrial cooperative agreement. An example is International Business Machines, which did not respond favorably to Romanian overtures toward establishing a joint association for production of computer-output printing equipment. Major U.S. corporations favor wholly owned subsidiaries; therefore, their involvement in the new opportunities offered by the European socialist countries is unlikely since this form of involvement is unacceptable to the host countries. The reason for the stand of the major U.S. corporations (whose assets are often multiples of the GNP of one single European socialist country) is that they are unwilling to adjust their production, distribution, and service to the strict conformity of plans and procedures determined by the host company.

In the developing countries, equity and nonequity ventures provide superior methods of channeling capital and know-how and of providing employment opportunities for local elites by maintaining the economic independence of the host countries. In these countries, the nonequity type of joint business venture is used increasingly since this form totally excludes the foreigner from any direct ownership in the business association. These contractual relations are often regarded by the governments of developing countries as the most proper form of association with developed industrial countries.

To sum up, the concept of the joint business venture is neither good nor bad. Its value depends on the degree to which it meets each partner's requirements. As with all business associations, the joint venture is created to carry on a business that will generate profits. These associations, therefore, cannot use their potentials if in host countries where an antibusiness climate exists.

It is known that the positive role of multinational corporations in the global system has not gone unchallenged. Critics assert that the Western investors use inappropriate technology in the host countries, destroy jobs, collect excess profits, and leave poverty and misery in their wake. Interestingly enough, none of these often-heard allegations are voiced by the European socialist countries that are seeking Western private direct investment. They generally believe that Western companies have a distinctive contribution to make to their socialist development. In this process they are ready to guarantee a probusiness climate.

## CASE STUDIES OF JOINT VENTURES

Studies, monographs, and books dealing with recent business ventures between socialist firms and their capitalist counterparts have multiplied at a greater rate than the joint undertakings themselves. The reason for this interest, both scholarly and practical, is understandable. The surprising 1967 Yugoslav decision,[3] which opened the door for business association with Western capitalist firms drew the attention of the world and, for many optimists, signaled new vistas after 25 years of cold war and confrontation. It was felt that improvements in political relationships could not only generate increased trade with the socialist countries but also create opportunities for such close economic undertakings as the joint venture in which local and Western managers would work side by side, sharing their daily burdens and pleasures and, last but not least, their profits.

Price-directed, worker-self-managed, market-socialist Yugoslavia was the first socialist country* to invite Western capital equity to incorporate in a joint undertaking. The abovementioned 1920 decree of Lenin notwithstanding, this move was unparalleled.

Everybody waited for the reactions of the other European socialist countries, and these, with the obvious exception of Albania,† were not unfavorable.

---

*With respect to travel regulations, the centrally planned Council for Mutual Economic Assistance (COMECON) countries exclude Yugoslavia from the socialist countries. Several Yugoslav protests have been lodged, but in vain.
†Radio Tirana broadcast: "Yugoslavia opens her door to Western monopolistic capital and subjects the Yugoslav economy to enslavement along with twofold increase of exploitation of domestic workers."[4]

The German Democratic Republic (GDR) and Czechoslovakia were among the first 11 foreign partners to conclude token joint venture contracts with Yugoslavia. The other countries of the COMECON group took the stand of expectation and exploration.

Romania was the first Soviet-bloc country to jump on the bandwagon. The Grand National Assembly of the Socialist Republic of Romania passed a bill on foreign trade and economic and technico-scientific cooperation activities.[5] Clarification followed shortly, and a subsequent bill dealing with questions of fiscal regulations and distribution of profits was passed by the State Council.[6]

After Romania, the second COMECON country to adopt a similar device was Hungary. The minister of finance issued a decree on economic association with foreign partners; no legislative action was necessary, as it had been in the former two countries, to make this rather important decision.[7]

## Yugoslavia

Yugoslavia has lived through many processes of socioeconomic change since 1965, which brought the introduction of numerous economic and social reforms. The changes have worked to develop the economy intensively and modernize it. The essence of this progress has been acceleration of the technical and technological reconstruction of industry, optimization of production capacity, specialization of production within the framework of the international division of labor, introduction of new engineering and technology, and integration of enterprises through formation of large production-commercial complexes designed to optimize production and financial results. The sum total of these activities has provided foundations for creating new opportunities and forms of lasting relationships between domestic enterprises and foreign partners.

In order to accomplish these changes, Yugoslavia created in 1965, in addition to promulgating the existing regulations concerning industrial cooperation, the institution of investment of foreign capital in domestic enterprises for the purpose of handling joint ventures in the area of production and trade, so that profit could be made while taking joint risk. As a result of changes in the constitution and in the corresponding laws and regulations, the legal security of capital investments as well as their repatriation have been fully guaranteed.

The principles and scope of enterprises in Yugoslavia having the partnership of foreign capital are determined by basic regulations concerning their creation, organization, and activities. The total value of the means that a foreign partner invests in a joint enterprise cannot exceed, or equal, the total sum of means invested by one, or several, domestic partners. Accordingly, the maximum share of foreign capital is 49 percent, with 51 percent in domestic capital. In exceptional cases, the Federal Parliament (Skupstina) can pass a special law allowing a greater proportion of capital to the foreign partner.

The means of the foreign partner cannot normally represent less than the equivalent sum of $100,000. The federal secretary for economic affairs can determine in what cases, depending on the type and nature of the activities, the investment of the foreign partner can be less than this amount.

In accordance with the Yugoslav law, relations under property law resulting from joint investments (ownership right, transfer of profits, and so on) are regulated by an agreement on joint enterprise. With regard to the invested means, the foreign partner does not have the right of ownership or of joint ownership. His right refers only to transfer of profits, repatriation of investment outlays, and transfer of amortized durable means of production brought to the enterprise. Investments in a joint enterprise can be of a nonfinancial as well as a financial nature. Investments in the form of nonfinancial means can consist of real estate (funds, buildings), movable property (such as equipment, various machines, semifinished products, reproduction material, and raw material), patent rights, licenses, know-how, technical documentation, and so on. The Yugoslav enterprise with foreign capital is a legal person and receives by analogy with other Yugoslav enterprises the constitutional right of using and freely disposing of means held jointly. The foreign partner has the right to transfer his rights and obligations resulting from the agreement to other legal or physical persons in a foreign country, or to a Yugoslav enterprise.

In the latter case, the foreign partner is obligated to submit in writing that he wishes to cede his share to the enterprise in which he has invested. If the enterprise turns down the offer, the partner can transfer his rights to other firms. The foreign partner can dispose of the entire amount of his profit. The profit of a foreign partner is subject to a tax of 35 percent. There are also provisions for various tax exemptions. For example, when 25 percent of the annual profit is assigned for increasing the shares, the exemption amounts to 15 percent; if the amount assigned is between 25 and 50 percent, the tax that is applicable to the amount in excess of 25 percent is reduced 30 percent; and if the amount assigned is more than 50 percent, the portion of the invested profit in excess of 50 percent is subject to a tax reduced by 50 percent.

The general director of a joint enterprise is always a Yugoslav citizen. The enterprise is created for a specific period of time, with the understanding that the time cannot be less than that needed for achieving the goals of the joint venture. Within the framework of the agreed time limit, the joint partners cannot cancel the contract by mutual agreement, let alone denounce it one-sidedly.

## Romania

In the Socialist Republic of Romania, the law on foreign trade and technico-scientific cooperation provides in article 58 that Romanian economic organizations, acting with the consent of competent organs, can establish mixed companies abroad as well as in Romania in the areas of industrial production, agricultural production, construction, communications, trade, scientific-technical research, and the services. Mixed companies are legal persons and act in accordance with the provisions of the Romanian law. The share of the capital on the Romanian part is to amount to 51 percent of total shares. The agreement on partnership is subject to registration in the Ministry of Foreign Trade, which determines whether the partnership is purposeful. The state, acting through authorized institutions, gives foreign partners a guarantee that amortization quotas and net profit can be transferred abroad. A special decree issued in 1972 concerning the creation, organization, and activities of mixed companies in Romania determined in detail the method of forming companies, their organization (joint stock companies or companies with limited responsibility), and the rights and obligations of the partners.

In determining the scope of a joint enterprise, the partners must consider the socioeconomic development trend in Romania. The state guarantees that the foreign partner can send abroad through the Romanian Foreign Trade Bank both his profits and the investments or rights resulting from dissolution of partnership if he has paid his taxes, fees, and social security dues and has complied with his legal and contractual obligations. The companies are obligated to prepare five-year as well as annual plans of economic and financial activities. The shares of the parties in the creation of the basic capital can apply to the financial share, durable as well as turnover means of production, and the share of industrial property rights. The share of the Romanian party can also include the equal value of the right of utilizing the terrain that the state places at the company's disposal for the period of its existence. In case the equal value of the right of using the terrain was not provided for in the share of the Romanian party, the company shall pay the state a rent based on the utilization of the terrain.

When acting for the purpose of establishing a partnerhsip, the partners are obligated to prepare in the Romanian language a document that justifies the technical-economic effectiveness of the joint venture, the contract, and the company's statutes. Before signing these documents, the Romanian partner must obtain approval from the State Planning Commission, the Ministry of Finance, and the Ministry of Foreign Trade, as well as from the bank that finances the venture. The Ministry of Foreign Trade submits the documents with its opinion to the Council of Ministers. Decisions concerning the creation of a company, the contract, and the statutes are confirmed by a decree of the state council at the motion of the Council of Ministers. The essential task of the joint company is production primarily for export purposes. The accounting of the company, in addition to minor administrative expenditures, purchases of goods, or payments for services for which the prices cannot be determined in terms of foreign currency, is done in leis.* The company's production that is sold on the domestic market is evaluated in a foreign currency that has been agreed to in the contract and on foreign markets directly or through the intermediary of foreign trade central offices. Bookkeeping concerning economic-financial transactions is done in a currency determined by the partners. The joint company has the right to employ foreign personnel, who can hold management functions. Disputes between companies and Romanian physical or legal persons are subject to the jurisdiction of the courts or, with the consent of the other party, to arbitration of the Arbitration Commission at the Romanian Chamber of Commerce.

The regulations described above in general terms have been supplemented by a decree of November 1972 concerning taxation of profits of joint enterprises. The State Council determined that profits gained by joint enterprises shall be taxed at the annual rate of 30 percent. At the same time, a reserve fund has been created in the amount of 5 percent of the profit. This fund is accumulated up to the amount of 25 percent of the invested capital. Tax reductions have been provided for, and also the possibility of periodic exemption of the company from taxes. In case a portion of the profit is allocated for additional investments over a period of at least five years, the tax is reduced by 20 percent. The remaining portion of the profit, after settlement of taxes, is taxed at the rate of 10 percent when transferred abroad.

## Hungary

In 1970, Hungary issued decree no. 17, with the strength of law, which concerns economic partnerships. The decree stipulates in section 31 that foreign legal persons, acting in agreement with the minister of finance, can participate in economic partnerships on Hungarian soil. A decree of the minister of finance, dated October 1972, regulates the formation of partnerships with participation of foreign capital. The partnership can be established on the basis of mutual interest of Hungarian and foreign partners for bringing about economic development of a commercial or service activity.

The capital investment of a western foreign partner cannot exceed 49

---

*Multiple exchange rates for the Romanian leu as of 1976 (lei per U.S. dollar) are as follows: Official (end of year): basic foreign trade rate—4.97; tourist and noncommercial rate—12.00. Black market (average of end of month): unlicensed transfers abroad—38.40.

percent; this rule is not applied to joint enterprises with foreign partners from socialist countries, and thus the Polish-Hungarian HALDEX company has proportional shares of 50 percent to 50 percent. A joint enterprise is obligated to create from profits a risk fund, which is to be increased each year until its sum reaches the amount of 10 percent of the company's property.

The company is obligated to pay an income tax based on its annual profit after deduction of risk fund and shareholders' fund. The amount of income tax is 40 percent if the profit does not exceed 20 percent of the value of the company's property and 60 percent when the profit exceeds 20 percent of the property. Tax deductions are provided when profit is invested in the enterprise.

Foreign workers employed by the company may send 50 percent of their income abroad in the foreign currency specified in the partnership agreement. The National Bank of Hungary can send abroad the profit belonging to the foreign partner as well as his other income in the foreign currency specified in the agreement. In case the foreign partner relinquishes his share in the company, the National Bank sends abroad the portion of the property corresponding to the partner up to the amount of the sums paid in the company's foreign currency. In case the company is liquidated, the portion of the foreign partner's property remaining after payment of debts is sent abroad without taxation.

The Hungarian legislation is based on the resolution of 1975 concerning administration of joint stock companies and public utilities, while, with regard to companies with limited responsibility, it is based on the law of 1930, amended by regulations of 1960 and 1970. The decree of the Hungarian minister of finance does not apply to matters regulated by international agreement. In view of the state monopoly in foreign trade, enterprises with participation of foreign capital, as with wholly Hungarian enterprises, can perform export-import transactions within a strictly limited scope and only with special permission of the Ministry of Foreign Trade.

## COMECON

Studies have been carried out by the Council for Mutual Economic Assistance designed to create appropriate legal and organizational conditions for joint economic activities. At its 25th session, COMECON adopted a complex program, which, among other things, obligated member countries to prepare normative acts pertaining to the establishment and activity of international economic organizations in the areas of production, trade, and scientific-technical cooperation. At the same time, COMECON adopted a recommendation for study of the possibility of multilateral agreements among COMECON countries. To carry out such study, the Council of Representatives of COME-

CON Member States for Legal Affairs appointed a special group of experts on international economic organizations.

Pursuant to the work of these experts, the COMECON Executive Committee prepared additional propositions as follows:

> Preparation of normative acts by member countries pertaining to the establishment and activity of international economic organizations as well as their legal position within the territory of the country where they are created;
> 
> Preparation of propositions concerning the establishment and activities of international economic organizations in those areas where there exist opportunities for applying uniform legal decisions as well as propositions of such decisions involving the possibility of signing multilateral agreements by the interested states.

On the basis of the existing regulations of socialist countries pertaining to enterprises with participation of foreign capital, including joint enterprises of socialist countries, one can discern common characteristics as well as trends toward uniformity of basic goals and organizational-legal decisions.

When joint ventures are proposed, the factor that is generally determined is whether the activities of the enterprise are in harmony with the economic goals of the host country, especially as regards the development of production for export purposes. The legal form in which most joint enterprises are approved is in either limited-responsibility or joint stock companies. Such companies are in the nature of a legal person and are subject to the legislature of the country where they are registered.

These companies are established either for a certain time period or without time limitation. The share of the domestic enterprise cannot be less than 51 percent of the basic capital. Government organs accordingly guarantee the return of investments to the foreign partner as well as the transfer of profit in the currency of the joint enterprise. Provisions are made for an increase of the basic capital through a system of tax exemptions. Under special circumstances, the enterprise can be entirely exempted from taxes. The income tax is determined within the limits of 30-40 percent of the net profit. Domestic enterprises can assign their property shares in the nature of investments other than monetary.

Enterprises with participation of foreign capital that are within the framework of the foreign trade monopoly of a socialist state operate on the basis of decisions of government organs responsible for the preservation of the monopoly—that is, primarily ministries of foreign trade, which issue the appropriate licenses for export and import activities. Such licenses are issued either directly or through domestic central offices of foreign trade. The agreement on a joint enterprise and its statutes is accepted or rejected in each case by government authorities on the basis of the anticipated benefit to the country.

One should note, however, that there is a gap between expected and realized benefits. The aggregate total foreign investment in Yugoslavia in the first five years (1967-72) totaled $143 million, which is just a little more than the cost of the Federal Bureau of Investigation's 1975 headquarters in Washington, D.C. Romania's contracts are similar, an example being the agreement with Control Data Corporation (headquarters in Minneapolis), where the foreign share is $.8 million. Hungary, similarly, has only token contracts.

A number of companies, especially in Yugoslavia, have felt that prospects and terms of agreement regarding enterprises with foreign investors were satisfactory, and they have found an advantage in sharing capital, technology, management, markets, risks, and profits. Other companies have been more cautious in their involvement.

## NOTES

1. This belief is reinforced by some United Nations' publications, which term joint venture a "recent" phenomenon replacing the wholly owned subsidiary corporation. See United Nations, *Manual on the Establishment of Industrial Joint Venture Agreements in Developing Countries* (New York: United Nations, 1971), p. 1.

2. Wolfgang G. Friedman and I. N. Pugh, *Legal Aspects of Foreign Investment* (Boston-Toronto, 1959), pp. 768-69.

3. *Official Gazette,* no. 31/1967, Federal Assembly of the Socialist Federal Republic of Yugoslavia, July 1967.

4. Radio Free Europe monitoring Radio Tirana on October 4, 1968, 3:30 p.m.

5. Bill no. 1, *Official Bulletin,* March 17, 1971.

6. Decree no. 425 on Tax and Profits of Joint Companies Constituted in the Socialist Republic of Romania, *Official Bulletin,* November 2, 1972.

7. Decree no. 28/1972, *Official Gazette of the People's Republic of Hungary* no. 76, October 3, 1972; see also *International Legal Materials* (4) 989, (1973).

# CHAPTER 4

## TAXATION OF THE FOREIGN SHARE IN COMMUNIST COUNTRIES

## YUGOSLAVIA

### The Market-Socialist System

Yugoslav theoreticians and politicians have been arguing that no communist party or country has the right to play a leading role within the international communist movement. They claim that there is no single road to socialism. The Yugoslav system is indeed a significantly different version of the Soviet-type model. On the basis of the constitution and the laws, Yugoslav enterprises are autonomous self-managed organizations, and they are entitled to assess freely all factors involved in entering into business arrangements. Enterprises may act as legal persons with full legal capacity. They are managed by the representatives of those (blue- and white-collar workers) who have established relationships with them. In spite of the fact the enterprises are subject to the control of the legality of their operations, basically they conform to market forces in accordance with the unique Yugoslav market-socialist system.

Yugoslav plans do not constitute legal, obligation-binding enterprises; they are mainly guidelines, similar to French plans. The enterprises are entitled to draw up their own development and investment plans.

The enterprises themselves distribute realized income and allocate it to various funds and to personal income (wages and salaries). Therefore, in Yugoslavia, checks on increasing wages are minimal, since the workers' councils decide wages, and the only limits are realized profits and contributions to various funds.

The manager is not appointed by the central authorities but is selected by the workers' council on the basis of competition. In the case of joint enterprise, the partners may agree that the foreign partner appoint an authorized person in his employ who would establish labor relationships with the enterprise. The title and capacity of this person is codirector, and he is not subject to the formal approval of the workers' council.

Yugoslavia, the nation of the South Slavic people, differs markedly in terms of its regions, and it is beneficial to understand the culture and traditions of its various peoples. The economic system is characterized by a pragmatic approach, and this method, in spite of its benefits, is probably responsible for the frequent switches and adjustments in economic policy.

Among the economic ills of the country, one should mention inflation coupled with unemployment. During 1960-70, the average rate of inflation was 12.1 percent. In 1971, the annual rate rose to 16 percent and in 1973 to 21 percent. In 1974, it reached 26 percent, and the estimated rate for 1975 was 30 percent.

Unemployment, which is widespread, started when the autonomous firms seeking profits released those workers who, in the form of "unemployment within the doors," represented an unnecessary labor surplus. During the first seven years of the New Economic Policy based on workers' self-management, the number of unemployed doubled. During the next seven years from 1964 to 1971, it almost doubled again, reaching 400,000. At the same time, 700,000 Yugoslav workers were permitted to seek employment in Western European countries, mainly in West Germany. With the economic slump in West Germany, however, these *Gastarbeiter* are coming home, adding to Yugoslavia's problems.

The federal government tries various stabilization policies but faces considerable difficulties.[1]

## Ownership

Equity is needed, under ordinary conditions, to establish a joint undertaking. Equity investment, in turn, is translated into ownership. If the equity comes from two or more partners, the business association should logically be in the form of co-ownership.

If one of the investors is from a Western country, and the joint business venture is in a socialist country, is this capitalist the partial owner of a socialist firm? This question presents a touchy problem. The most vitriolic rhetoric originating from persons of Marxist persuasion is directed against the various forms of exploitation of the Western monopoly capital. It does indeed seem contradictory that countries that, in accordance with the prescription of socialist theories, expropriated the property of their own capitalists who owned the factors of production are now inviting the cooperation of Western entrepreneurs in order to pocket the Marxian "surplus value"—that is, the profits. It seems that Yugoslav theorists were much concerned to provide an acceptable solution for this puzzle, Yugoslavia being the first socialist country to accept Western investors and its leaders being apprehensive of criticism from the COMECON group. It is interesting that this criticism was not forthcoming and, moreover, that political leaders and ideologists in Romania and Hungary were considerably less sensitive to the question than their Yugoslav counterparts.

The Yugoslav solution of the problem is both complex and elegant and may provide a blueprint for all those nations that badly need foreign capital in order to solve some of their economic ills but, at the same time, are hesitant to invite foreign capital into their economy. Yugoslav theoreticians propose that at the very moment the foreign capital crosses the border of the country, it becomes socially owned. It is claimed that the foreign capital coming from Western investors, *in iure,* is not associated with capitalist assets in the socialist country since the capitalists are not co-owners of the assets of the joint undertakings.

This solution is derived from a concept of Roman law, namely from the term *instituta pactum reservati domini.* This is practiced in trade as a sort of security for the seller that the buyer will fulfill the contract. A car remains in the ownership of the dealer until all the payments are made, but it is operated and used by the buyer. Similarly, the foreign investor can use the whole part of his share, but he does not own it due to an assumed virtual obligation to the socialist state. He retains the title to his invested assets, but this does not violate Article 8 of the federal constitution, which lays down the principle that "no one has the ownership to the social means of production and that the means of production and other means of social work ... are social property." The word "ownership" was also carefully left out in the entire foreign investment legislation. (The Hungarian decree speaks about the "foreign partner's share" in paragraph 11/4; the Romanian decree speaks about the "share of the parties" in several places.)

The rights of the foreign investor, in spite of the fact that he does not own any assets in the Yugoslav economy, seem quite secure. The regulations provide that he may share in the profits from the joint venture "as long as he participates in it with his own assets" and also that he has the right to return the particular items invested in the joint venture. The foreign investor, therefore, subject to the contract, could retrieve his entire equity regardless of what it consisted of (cash, tangibles, intangibles); practice has demonstrated and confirmed this option. Therefore, a piece of machinery that has a lifetime of ten years can have an interesting curriculum. Used by a foreign investor as equity in a Yugoslav investment, it becomes socially owned property, but if the investor returns home after five years the machine again becomes private property. It seems that these metamorphoses bother neither the machines nor the investors, who consider their ownership in the assets of the Yugoslav joint venture as a de facto case.

## Restrictions on Foreign Investments

Host governments often impose limits and restrictions on foreign investments, and regulations are often made that exclude foreign capital from certain areas of activity. Most countries exclude foreign investments in some strategic and vital industries, such as public utilities, coastal shipping, radio and television broadcasting, public transportation, and electric power distribution. National legislation usually applies to four different groups of activity: those reserved for the state only; involvements of local citizens and local corporations not having foreign shareholders; activities requiring over 50 percent of local capital; and activities not restricting foreign participation in ownership or management.

The Yugoslav approach is the following: Banking, insurance, inland transportation, internal commerce, public utilities, and social services are areas or sectors in which all foreign investment is excluded. An exception can be made by the Federal Executive Council if it decides that a particular investment will expedite the development of a certain sector. So far, the council has not used its powers in this respect although potential foreign investors have been interested in entering into complex projects involving inland transportation.

Some sectors, such as manufacturing, processing, the extractive industries, agriculture, tourism, and research, are open for foreign participation and for registration with the government. It is also a possibility, although highly unlikely, that, on the basis of a special act of the Federal Assembly, minority participations in these propulsive sectors might be converted into majority participation.

A special territorially determined area of foreign investment is a custom-free zone. In Yugoslavia, nine such zones have been registered: Belgrade, Novi Sad, Rijeka, Koper, Split, Zadar, Ploce, Bar, and Pula. Article 2 of the respective decree enumerates activities using foreign equipment that may be jointly run within these zones: storage of goods, perfection of foreign goods, usual handling of goods such as classifying and packaging, and erection and financing of other facilities.

The absence of any joint investment in a zone indicates that the legislation may be too restrictive. Now an amendment of that legislation has been initiated. Proposals call for legislation allowing, in addition to the listed activities, industrial manufacture coupled with custom-free import of foreign-invested equipment. Such proposals of three ports (Belgrade, Rijeka, and Koper) have been backed by the Assemblies of the Socialist Republic of Croatia and the Socialist Republic of Slovenia. Table 4.1 shows Yugoslav joint ventures by

## TABLE 4.1

### Yugoslav Joint Ventures by Foreign Partner's Country and Contribution as of January 7, 1973

| Country of Foreign Partner | Number of Ventures | Foreign Contribution | Percent of Total Foreign Investment | Percent of Total Joint Investment |
|---|---|---|---|---|
| Austria | 3 | $8,188,373 | 5.744 | 1.18 |
| Belgium | 3 | 2,540,345 | 1.780 | 0.36 |
| Czechoslovakia | 1 | 6,484,480 | 4.550 | 0.93 |
| Denmark | 1 | 304,640 | 0.220 | 0.04 |
| England | 2 | 796,676 | 0.560 | 0.11 |
| Federal Republic of Germany | 16 | 29,091,564 | 20.410 | 4.17 |
| France | 4 | 9,917,776 | 6.960 | 1.42 |
| German Democratic Republic | 1 | 15,047,040 | 10.560 | 2.16 |
| Italy | 19 | 35,588,379 | 24.960 | 5.11 |
| Japan | 1 | 66,640 | 0.050 | 0.01 |
| Netherlands | 1 | 1,502,389 | 1.050 | 0.22 |
| Sweden | 2 | 5,752,591 | 4.030 | 0.83 |
| Switzerland | 10 | 6,339,725 | 4.450 | 0.91 |
| United States | 3 | 2,968,035 | 2.080 | 0.43 |
| Financial Organizations | | | | |
| DEG | 1 | 772,059 | 0.54 | 0.11 |
| IICY | 2 | 1,106,779 | 0.77 | 0.16 |
| IFC | 4 | 16,092,249 | 11.29 | 2.31 |

| | Domestic | Foreign | Total |
|---|---|---|---|
| Grand total | $554,166,483 | $142,559,740 | $696,726,223 |

*Note:* DEG (Deutsche Entwicklungsgesellschaft); IFC (International Finance Corporation).

*Source:* International Investment Corporation for Yugoslavia (IICY).

foreign partner. Table 4.2 lists geographical distribution within Yugoslavia of foreign capital.

## Taxation of Joint Ventures

### Gross Income, Net Income, and Profit

Joint venture contracts in Yugoslavia have adopted the same systems of income formation, computation of profits, and accountancy as all domestic

## TABLE 4.2

### Geographical Distribution of Foreign Invested Capital Within Yugoslavia as of January 7, 1973

| Location | Number of Ventures | Foreign Contribution (in U.S. $) | Percent of Total Foreign Investment | Percent of Total Joint Investment |
|---|---|---|---|---|
| Bosnia and Herzegovina | 6 | 9,940,134 | 6.97 | 1.34 |
| Croatia | 15 | 10,961,004 | 7.69 | 1.57 |
| Macedonia | 3 | 5,250,239 | 3.68 | 0.75 |
| Montenegro | 1 | 3,124,716 | 2.19 | 0.45 |
| Serbia | 19 | 58,089,591 | 40.75 | 8.34 |
| – Serbia without provinces | 14 | 54,909,119 | 38.52 | 7.88 |
| – S.A. province of Kosovo | 2 | 1,158,387 | 0.81 | 0.16 |
| – S.A. province of Vojvodina | 3 | 2,022,085 | 1.42 | 0.30 |
| Slovenia | 27 | 55,194,056 | 38.72 | 7.92 |

*Note:* Amounts include investments by Deutsche Entwicklungsgesellschaft (DEG), International Investment Corporation for Yugoslavia (IICY), and International Finance Corporation (IFC).

*Source:* International Investment Corporation for Yugoslavia.

enterprises. Accordingly, gross income is the total receipt accrued from invoiced sales of product and services. This figure, diminished by the material costs and services bought and the amount of depreciation of fixed assets (domestic and foreign), is net income, or simply income. In other words, income is the difference between gross income and the cost of material and services and depreciation.

Material costs and services are enumerated in the Law of Formation and Computation of Total Receipts and Income in the Basic Organizations of Associate Work, published in the *Official Gazette* of the Socialist Federal Republic (SFR) of Yugoslavia, nos. 71/72, p. 1427. In accordance with this regulation, these include raw and other materials used, services of third parties, rent, advertising and promotion, participation in fairs, receipts of clients, maintenance of fixed assets, purchase of protective devices and clothing for workers, transportation for workers, and emoluments of apprentices. The Western reader may be astonished not to find labor costs in this enumeration. Under worker self-management, labor costs are not considered expenditures since they are received by the "owners" of the enterprise.

Outside of wages and salaries and contributions on personal incomes, legal and contractual reservations * are additional oblications. The remainder is the distributable profit.

## Distribution of Profit

For distribution of profit, the law is flexible. The foreign partner can take his share out in accordance with his percentage of equity in total assets, whereas the domestic partner can use his share in two ways: for salary/wage bonuses and for allocation to the enterprise's funds.

A warning to the foreign investor, however, is in order. There is a possibility that the net income will be further diminished by allocation to the enterprise funds prior to distribution to the parties. This question should be outlined clearly in the contract and approved by the workers' council. In any case, a special tax is levied on the foreign shares, after which the share becomes transferable.

Consequently, there have been two categories of tax at large: (1) the shared tax and (2) the profit tax affecting the foreign partner only. The shared taxes affect all the deductions from income in the forms of legal reservations, contractual reservations, and contributions on paid personal incomes. This means that the foreigner's portion of the profits, prior to being specially taxed as such, passes through all the same deductions as the domestic partner's portion. Then the foreigner pays his own tax separately to the host country, and, if the country does not have a tax treaty with the investor's country of origin, he pays taxes the third time at home.

It is true that the foreign investor often need not pay all the obligations that remain after the computation of net income, but this stipulation remains on the contract, and it should be outlined to what extent he will participate in these expenditures. Therefore, the contract should define clearly the standards on production material and manpower expenditures, and, in addition, general expenses and their methods of computation. The foreign partner would be right to reject computation of shared expenses over and above the standards set in advance. Also, it is up to the parties to decide beforehand whether and to what extent the foreigner will share in contributing to the division's fund and to its commitments to the parent's reserves. These additional contributions are not mandatory, unlike the legal reserves of economic organizations, which are among legal withholdings.

---

*Legal reservations affecting income include contribution for the use of urban ground; water rate; turnover tax; and contribution for mandatory joint reserves of economic organizations paid to the commune or republic within which the enterprise is located. Contractual reservations affecting income include loan and interest payments; insurance premiums; bankers' commissions; membership fees to chambers, associations, and so on.

The next question concerns losses. The contracts provide that the parties will share in the losses in proportion to their investments. However, one common feature is apparent: In either case, the losses could be written off as tax deductible.

The law does not require that the shares in net distributable profits be proportionate to each partner's contribution, but, in practice, all contracts concluded so far demonstrate that the equity ratio was the sole criterion for such a distribution.

## Tax Holidays

The Yugoslav federal legislation does not grant any tax holidays following the first year of profits, although many foreign investors want this. However, it grants a concessionary reduction of the initial 35 percent in proportion to the percentage of profit that the foreign investor plugs back. The rate is reduced on a sliding scale. In other words, as the reinvestment rises, the reduction increases. The foreigner enjoys the same concession if he banks the same percentages of his profits for longer than ten years. If the deposit is for at least five years, the concession is half. The tax concessions are not applied if the withdrawal period is less than five years. Interest on the deposit of the foreigner's profit is not taxable.

## Withholding Tax Affecting the Foreign Partner

It was concluded in the previous section that shared taxes are treated as an expense of the joint venture and that profit taxes are paid solely by the foreign partner. Is there a form of tax that affects the Yugoslav partner alone? Possibly. There is the mandatory loan to the underdeveloped areas of Yugoslavia, but this can occur only if the contract excuses the foreign partner from liability for it. The foreign partner, in general, does not escape from any tax payment that affects his Yugoslav counterpart.

Analysis of the shared taxes reveals that presently the income (earnings) of the Yugoslav enterprise is not taxed. What is taxed is the payroll (workers' personal income—that is, wages/salaries). In the future, however, sweeping changes are expected in the field of taxation. The republics became responsible for tax legislation pursuant to constitutional changes, and they are expected to modify, change, and reverse the present taxation patterns. The tax laws of the various republics differ widely, and foreign investors should be aware of local regulations, which are different, for example, in the Socialist Republics of Serbia and of Bosnia-Herzegovina.[2]

All shared taxes affect the distributable profit and, consequently, the foreign partner's portion of it, on which is levied a subsequent 35 percent tax.

This portion has been subject to all the initial taxes and has diminished accordingly.

The foreign partner, having licensed some patents against royalty payments, capitalizes the received payments; the latter is subject to the same rate. In accordance with United States tax regulations, the United States investor by capitalizing his patents in another country earns additional income; therefore, he is normally also subject to taxation for the same royalty in his home country.

The Yugoslav partner-enterprise calculates and effects the payment of this withholding tax for the foreign coventurer and accordingly subtracts it from the foreigner's share of the profit. From what was said above, it should be clear that the 35 percent profit tax affects only the foreigner's share of profits. The taxation is executed by monthly estimated payments during the calendar year, unless the recipient enterprise draws its balance sheets quarterly. Both partners are held liable for any failure to pay the tax.

As mentioned above, all the republics, both developed and undeveloped, are now entitled to tax foreign investors according to their statutes. So far, all the developed republics have passed laws on taxes payable by foreign persons. These republics are Serbia, Slovenia, and Croatia. The laws relate to joint ventures, performance of construction, turnkey jobs,* and transportation. The Serbian and Slovenian laws provide a 35 percent tax rate on the foreigner's profit from joint investment. The Croatian law sets forth that the rates will be proportional or will be set individually by communal assemblies.

Reports of the Communal Revenue Offices of the Croatian Communal Assemblies were sent to the Institute of International Politics and Economics in Belgrade. There, a tabulation was made and a copy was given by Dr. Miodrag Sukijasovic to the present author. The tabulation showed the following tax rates for Croatia:

> 35 percent (Beli, Manastir, Benkovas, Biograd na moru, Bjelovar, Buje, Buzet, Cakovec, Daruvar, Delnice, Donji, Lapac, Duga, Resa, Dugo, Dvor, Durdevac, Garesnica, Glina, Grubisino Polje, Imotzki, Ivaned, Ivanic-Grad, Knin, Koprivnica, Korcula, Karpina, Krizevci, Krk, Kutina, Mali Losinj, Metkovic, Novska, Nova Gradiska, Opatija, Osijek, Rijeka, Samobor, Senj, Sisak, Slavonska Pozega, Slavonski Brod, Split, Titova Korenica, Trogir, Umag, Valpovo, Varazdin, Vinkovci, Virovitica, Vrbobsko, Vukovar, Zadar, Zagreb.)
>
> 20 percent, Dubrovnik: Within the province of the commune Labin, if the investment is in substitution of mining activity, the regular 35 percent

---

*A turnkey job is a project managed from the beginning to the end by the foreign partner. At the end the keys are given to the contractor who takes over the finished plant.

rate will be reduced to 20 percent. Some communal assemblies have not decreed on this matter as yet.

All the underdeveloped republics and the undeveloped province of Kosovo have also passed statutes. Concerning the foreigner's profit from joint investment, the Bosnian-Herzegovinian law provides for a 20 percent tax rate; under the Macedonian law, the rate is 14 percent. Kosovo's Law on Taxation of Foreign Persons, as far as joint investment is concerned, follows the 1969 Montenegrin Law on Profit Tax Concessions Favoring Foreign Persons Investing in a Domestic Organization for Running Business in Common. The tax rate is 35 percent. However, if the foreign partner reinvests more than 20 percent of the profits earned in one year, the nominally assessed tax (35 percent) on the difference between the 20 percent and the actually invested figure will be diminished by 90 percent. (Article 8). If the foreign partner banks more than 20 percent of his annual profits in the autonomous province of Kosovo with a withdrawal period not less than three years, the 35 percent tax will be lowered by 80 percent. International investment corporations for Yugoslavia are exempted, under the same conditions as those laid down in the Bosnian-Herzegovinian, Croatian, Macedonian, Serbian, and Slovenian laws, from tax on profits earned from investment within Kosovo province.

## Taxation of Citizens and Foreign Nationals

The title is redundant since, according to Yugoslav legislation, the term "citizen" means every citizen of the country or civil juridical person and every foreign national and foreign private juridical person whose income is over a specified amount.

The present form of taxation of citizens was introduced in 1968 and has been revised a number of times. The revisions indicate two trends in the tax policies of Yugoslavia: (1) increasing application of the concept of progression and (2) shifting of responsibility for taxation to the republics and municipalities from the federal government. In this process of change, considerable conflict can be detected; moreover, not all the laws have been codified.

Until 1968, setting rates on personal income tax was the responsibility of federal law. As revenue, it was left from the outset to the municipalities *(opstinas)*, although officially the federation was entitled to it. Since the constitutional amendments of 1971, it has been within the jurisdiction of the republics and autonomous provinces.

Yugoslav tax experts argue that to follow all the rules of taxation in Yugoslavia is almost impossible but that decentralization in such a country makes considerable sense. The reason, they propose, is that the country consists of areas that are widely different in terms of personal earnings. In Slovenia, per capita incomes are only slightly lower than in Austria, while the undeveloped autonomous province of Kosovo is considered by many to be one of the most depressed areas in Europe. Regions vary considerably in demographic indicators which indirectly affect personal income taxes.

At present, all the republics and autonomous provinces have enacted income tax regulations. Viewed as a whole, theory does not vary significantly. As an expected outcome, the legislations of the developed republics of Slovenia and Croatia and the developed autonomous province of Voivodina, are the most sophisticated, leaving little room for loopholes. The system of Yugoslav decentralization has gone a little bit far, however, even if one accepts the tax experts' explanation for the policy of differential taxation. One can hardly justify the existence of 184 tax areas in a single country of relatively modest size. The existing situation creates many disputes that are often unsolvable or whose complicated nature creates serious misallocation in the administrative and legal establishments.

The object of taxation in the 184 tax areas seems to be uniform: The tax is levied on income generated from personal income tax of permanent employees, on receipts from agricultural activity, on royalties (including patents and technical improvement), and on self-employment in the professions, crafts, and trades. Income from property such as buildings and property rights is included in the tax base, and the proceeds from pensions are also taxable.

Foreign nationals enjoy a special status in Croatia. It is explicitly stated in the tax legislation of Croatia that the profits of foreign nationals (physical persons or private juridical persons) that originate from investment in a local production process are not to be included in the object of taxation and are therefore tax free. At present, in all communities, there seem to be no taxes imposed on remittances of dividends or interest on royal royalties originating from abroad.

## A Comparative Survey of Yugolsav Income Taxation

Differences do exist, of course, in taxation policy in the steepness of progression, the level of nontaxable amount, the level of deduction for dependents, types and level of other deductions, and, especially, the size of the tax burden on total income. These differences occur not only among the republics and provinces but also among various opstinas in Serbia.

Republic laws have altogether exempted from taxation incomes based on decorations and veterans' supplements; the holders of the 1941 Partisan Medal (awarded to those who fought in Partisan resistance as early as 1941) are also exempted from some taxes. The taxpayer is always an individual, and he is taxed according to the place of his permanent residence. This applies to Yugoslavs working in Yugoslav missions or branch offices abroad and to the earnings of foreign nationals employed in a Yugoslav work organization.

The tax base always consists of the "object of taxation" minus taxes and contributions paid on individual sources of income; also deductible are a specified amount established by regulation known as the "nontaxable amount" and, as well, specified amounts for dependents. Taxes and contributions paid on sources of income are eliminated from the total income by a certain automatic technical tax procedure in the actual amounts computed and paid.

The nontaxable amount has been set at varying levels. Table 4.3 shows the situation in 1973.

Slovenia has a general rule for the nontaxable amount. It equals the average personal income of employed persons; therefore, the fiscal policy of this republic can be summarized as no income tax for those who earn the average income. In other republics and provinces, this exemption looks much higher than the average income. In the nonlisted republics (and autonomous provinces), the nontaxable amount has not been objectified yet, and it varies every year. It is pegged to the cost-of-living index in Serbia, to the average increments in nominal personal incomes in Macedonia, and to other ad hoc established indicators in the other republics.

The system of deductions has also been established in different ways. Montenegro and Serbia have simple deductions; elsewhere they are more complex. By far the most important deduction is for dependents, and these amounts are as follows:

*Serbia:* Deductions are prescribed by opstinas and amount to about 3,000 dinars\* per dependent. There is usually a maximum total amount of deduc-

## TABLE 4.3
### Nontaxable Amount, 1973

| Republics | Dinars |
|---|---|
| Serbia and autonomous provinces | 30,000–40,000 |
| Montenegro | 39,000 |
| Bosnia-Herzegovina | 37,000 |
| Croatia | 35,000 |
| Macedonia | 30,000 |
| Slovenia | 25,000 |

*Source:* National Bank of Yugoslavia, *Quarterly Bulletin.*

---

\*Multiple exchange rates for the Yugoslav dinar as of 1976 (dinar per U.S. dollar) are as follows:

Official (end of year): official rate—17.00; effective rate—18.18.

Black market (average of end of month): unlicensed transfers abroad—19.15.

tions (8,000 to 12,000 dinars). Only taxpayers in the family who are themselves gainfully employed may take advantage of them;

*Montenegro:* Deductions amount to 4,000 dinars per dependent, and the maximum is 16,000 dinars. They may be used only by taxpayers in the household or family who are gainfully employed;

*Slovenia:* Deductions amount to 12,000 dinars for every dependent child or 10,000 dinars for another dependent member of the family. Should any of them obtain income, the deduction is reduced by the amount of income. The deductions are recognized regardless of the number of family or household members who are gainfully employed; as a rule, they are applied to the total income of that member who had the highest earnings. If his total income cannot absorb the entire deduction, the total income of any other member of the family or taxpayer is diminished by the difference;

*Croatia:* The situation is much the same as in Slovenia, with two essential differences: First, a taxpayer whose total income does not exceed 18,000 dinars per family member is entitled to the deductions; second, opstinas are authorized to prescribe deductions on the basis of investments in construction or adaptation of business premises, purchase of equipment, and so on, which is not the case in Slovenia;

*Macedonia:* 5,000 dinars per member of the household or family is acknowledged for maintenance of spouse and children. Should any of them have income, the deduction is diminished by that amount;

*Bosnia-Herzegovina:* It is generally established that exemptions for dependents will be acknowledged in an amount to be established by separate law, which has not yet been enacted.

Republic statutes (and communal, or opstina, statutes in Serbia) have also established other exemptions, but these are not so important in the system of Yugoslav taxation. They include expenses for child support by court order, for maintaining elderly parents in public institutions (in Slovenia), for patenting inventions and products that have not been purchased, for anniversary celebrations for top-level political or cultural figures, and for defense of master's or doctoral dissertations; they also include earnings of the members of the Academy of Sciences and Arts in Belgrade, and so on.

Without exception, the tax rates are progressive. The progression is by brackets and ranges from 2 to 90 percent (see Table 4.4).

Judging by the method of establishing the individual elements of this tax, we can speak about a rather high degree of unity in spite of the pluralism in the system. But if we look at the extreme results (the tax burden on total income of a particular amount), we would be more inclined to speak of total disunity. To be sure, this disunity results from current tax policy, which is not important to the payer of the tax.

Table 4.5 shows how this burden is computed for a sample family with a varying number of members in which there is one breadwinner.

## TABLE 4.4

### Minimum and Maximum Base Tax Rates
### (in dinars)

| Socialist Republic | Minimum Base Rate | | Maximum Base Rate | |
|---|---|---|---|---|
| | Base (up to) | Rate | Base (over) | Rate |
| Croatia | 7,000 | 3 | 120,000 | 70 |
| Slovenia | 5,000 | 2 | 150,000 | 90 |
| Macedonia | 5,000 | 3 | 80,000 | 75 |
| Bosnia-Herzegovina | 10,000 | 3 | 80,000 | 70 |
| Montenegro | 5,000 | 3 | 50,000 | 80 |
| Serbia (Belgrade) | 5,000 | 3 | 100,000 | 70 |

*Source:* National Bank of Yugoslavia, *Quarterly Bulletin.*

## TABLE 4.5

### Tax Burden, for Two-to-Four-Member Families

| Socialist Republic | Amount of the Tax on This Total Income, in Dinars | | | |
|---|---|---|---|---|
| | 50,000 | 60,000 | 70,000 | 80,000 |
| I. Two-member family: | | | | |
| Bosnia-Herzegovina | 228 | 834 | 1,980 | 4,050 |
| Montenegro | 250 | 1,040 | 2,750 | 6,300 |
| Macedonia | 650 | 1,600 | 3,200 | 5,650 |
| Croatia | 630 | 1,450 | 2,660 | 4,510 |
| Slovenia | 450 | 1,150 | 2,450 | 4,350 |
| Serbia (Belgrade) | 240 | 930 | 2,250 | 4,100 |
| II. Three-member family: | | | | |
| Bosnia-Herzegovina | 66 | 432 | 1,314 | 2,840 |
| Montenegro | 90 | 640 | 1,910 | 4,700 |
| Macedonia | 350 | 1,050 | 2,500 | 4,300 |
| Croatia | — | 1,450 | 2,660 | 4,510 |
| Slovenia | — | 370 | 990 | 2,130 |
| Serbia (Belgrade) | 120 | 675 | 1,800 | 3,500 |
| III. Four-member family: | | | | |
| Bosnia-Herzegovina | — | 240 | 767 | 1,920 |
| Montenegro | — | 350 | 1,280 | 3,250 |
| Macedonia | 150 | 650 | 1,600 | 3,200 |
| Croatia | — | 210 | 770 | 4,510 |
| Slovenia | — | 60 | 370 | 990 |
| Serbia (Belgrade) | 30 | 450 | 1,350 | 2,900 |

*Source:* National Bank of Yugoslavia, *Quarterly Bulletin.*

When the differences in the tax burden resulting from this tax are as they are shown through the example of a family with one breadwinner, it is not difficult to imagine that these differences are greater for a family with two breadwinners (since in this case the deductions are not recognized in most republics). Unfortunately, it is not possible here to provide other figures.

*A Critique of the Yugoslav System of Personal Taxation*

If one agrees that one main goal of personal taxes—outside of the income-generating effect for municipalities and other governments—is to correct shortcomings in income distribution, then the Yugoslav system seems rather limited. The relatively large nontaxable amount in most cases is over the average income in the community, and this leaves little room to correct differences around the median income ranges, which are probably associated with the highest frequencies, that is, the largest group of citizens.

Certain preconditions need to be met by basic taxation if the principal function of the tax from total income is to be performed more fully. First, income and proceeds must be ascertained accurately, objectively, and according to uniform criteria. This is not the case in Yugoslavia. On the contrary, some are accurately recorded (income from permanent employment and others), while others are ascertained arbitrarily and depending on the capabilities of tax authorities (self-employment), and still others are objectified. Actually this question ought to be the point of departure for additional work on the system of taxation of total income. After all, basic taxation should determine the nature of supplementary taxation, and supplementary taxation should reflect the character of basic taxation.

Second, two or more progressions should not be applied to the same income. Basic taxation should be done with proportional rates and supplementary taxation with progressive rates, and the supplemental tax must be more comprehensive. In Yugoslavia, certain earnings (such as those of farmers, craftsmen, and tradesmen and proceeds from buildings) are progressively taxed twice, though there is no reason for this. We say there is no reason because in Serbia, for example, only 20 percent of total direct payments by farmers are computed by progressive rates. This is a consequence of the high share of various contributions in the structure of payments whose rates are proportional. Much the same is the case with other categories of taxpayers.

Third, basic taxation ought not to be excessively reduced with various deductions and exemptions from total income. There are grounds for believing that economically motivated deductions should be acknowledged at the point of basic taxation, while socially motivated deductions should be recognized at the point of supplemental (total) taxation.

Fourth, territorial differences in the level of the burden of basic taxes borne by the various sources of income ought not to be so great that supplemental taxation cannot objectively correct them. The uniformity of the corrective effect ought to be derived from the constitutional rights and obligations of citizens, the unity of the market, and the interest (in the broadest sense of the word) of citizens paying taxes to pay the same tax and other obligations on the same income.

The nontaxable amount is obviously the element most open to dispute. It is anonymous and undefined. It seems to be a legacy from the time when this tax was paid by a small number of taxpayers, precisely those who were in a position to shape the system. Its only purpose is to diminish the effect of the tax, and this can also be achieved through tax rate policy. Indirectly, it does diminish the paper work, but for this very reason its coverage is inadequate (it affects a small number of taxpayers). It is related to a total income that in itself is defective (differences in determination of income, exemptions, differences in the way individual sources of income are taxed), and it therefore has very few results and limited effect. How otherwise to interpret the fact that in Serbia there are only 48,323 taxpayers, which constitute 4 percent of all permanently employed persons and 2 percent of the total number of taxpayers of all categories? This group includes only five farmers, though there are 750,000 farmers who pay taxes; 95 lawyers, though there are 1,152 offices of self-employed attorneys; and 233 self-employed craftsmen and tradesmen, though there are 34,410 registered craft and trade establishments. It would be helpful if the nontaxable amount were eliminated, as it is both a fiction and the greatest error in the Yugoslav income tax system.

# ROMANIA

## A Strict Centrally Planned System

Romania, the maverick of the Soviet bloc, conducts her foreign relations more or less independently of the Soviet Union and the rest of the COMECON countries; at the same time, she maintains a tight grip on her domestic economy, which is one of the strictest centrally planned systems in East Europe. Enterprise self-management (auto-conducive) is inconceivable and control over enterprises has been strengthened.

Romania is the fastest growing country in the COMECON group, and her current economic plans provide for further impressive increases in industrial production. In accordance with Stalinist development policy, heavy industry is emphasized at the expense of consumer goods production. The planned average rate of industrial expansion is 32–34 percent for 1976–80. Thus, Romania not only has the highest "accumulation" rate in Eastern Europe but also is apparently determined to push it higher with every annual plan.

Among the industrial sectors, as expected, the rate of expansion of heavy industry is more than double that of the light and food industries.

From 1975 economic plans are far more detailed than their predecessors. For instance, the table on industrial production targets now contains over 20 new items, the table on agricultural production has been filled out, and the new table shows the irrigated areas for various crops. In addition, several other sections have been expanded.

The planned increases in national defense are far higher than in recent years. Foreign trade trends may explain this pattern. Romania's total trade with COMECON and "other socialist countries" decreases, while trade with the United States, the Common Market, and less developed countries increases. These figures demonstrate that Romania is determined to guard her relative independence but that, in order to do this, she follows the "super-industrialization" concept that dominated Soviet economic policies during the Stalinist period. This requires that ideological screws be tightened and that more and more sacrifices be demanded from the population.[3]

The difficulties of the Romanian economy include (1) a low rate of efficiency: In the current plans, 70 percent of the industrial production is to come from higher labor productivity rather than new investment; the concern with efficiency has been expressed frequently and at very high levels, and First Party Secretary Nicolae Ceausescu frequently discusses this theme; (2) apathy and carelessness among the workers: This is likely due to continued emphasis on overfulfilling ambitious production goals, lack of incentives, and limited remuneration for the workers despite economic progress achieved; accidents have occurred and major damages have been sustained in several parts of Romanian heavy industry; the apparent cause of these accidents was workers' carelessness; and (3) slow increase in the standard of living: One indication of this was to be found in the presentation of the draft 1976–80 plan; political leaders went to great lengths to explain that a high rate of growth in production goods was necessary to achieve an increase of consumer goods; there are also recent reports of food hoarding since basic food products are not readily available.

## Ownership

The equity invested in Romanian firms, in accordance with Decree no. 425 on Tax and Profits of Joint Companies Constituted in the Socialist Republic of Romania, November 2, 1972, represents a fundamental change in the earlier Romanian position, which demanded "exclusive ownership of all joint economic units established in Romania." The 1972 decree was an attempt to introduce new methods designed to alleviate the chronic deficit in Romania's trade balance, especially vis-a-vis the Western industrialized nations. It was hoped that joint ventures with Western companies would contribute considerably to improving this situation, but it was clear that Romania had to grant adequate guarantees in order to make investment an attractive proposition.

The draft law on foreign trade of February 1971 included two articles that dealt briefly with cooperation between Romanian and foreign organizations. Due to the importance of joint ventures, the original draft of the law related to this particular issue underwent substantial amendments in the final text published in March 1971. (Articles nos. 57 and 58 were extended, and two new articles, nos. 59 and 60, were added.) Although the final text of the law guaranteed foreign partners the right to transfer quotas of output, profits, and other amounts due to them, foreign firms remained reluctant to enter into cooperative ventures with Romanian firms because many important details had never been established clearly enough by law.

The seven chapters of Decree no. 424 deal with setting up the organization and the functioning of mixed companies in Romania. In Chapter 1, the guarantees that are granted to foreign partners for the transfer of quotas, profits, and so on, are reiterated. Chapter 2 deals with juridical matters related to the founding of joint ventures, contracts between partner's statutes, and the contributions of the partners.

## Taxation of Joint Ventures

### Determination of Gross Income, Net Income, and Profits

The accounts of the joint venture are not kept in the local currency but in the so-called agreed currency. (Some minor exceptions to this rule are enumerated in Article 21, but they need not concern us.) The "agreed currency," although not stated explicitly, is usually the currency of the foreign partner. If the foreign partner's country lacks convertible currency, then the accounts are kept in a selected hard currency. The reason for this is relatively simple. In a centrally planned economy, actual prices are distorted (over or underpriced), and they reflect not relative scarcities but, rather, the decisions of the central planning bureaus. To generate economic growth, this authority overprices consumer goods and underprices capital goods and various inputs. Romanian authorities rightly feel that it would be unfair to sponsor the operation of a joint venture from the sacrifices of the Romanian population, which would be required to maintain an artificially low price level on input prices.

The association is separated from the actual prices of the local markets; therefore, it cannot have any lei expenses. The wages of local employees and any domestic supply price will be paid by the Romanian authorities in lei, and the joint venture is not concerned. How, then, are costs arising from the usage of domestic resources determined? The unit price of the domestic inputs should be negotiated in the contract in terms of the hard currency selected.

The bill will come from the state authorities and not from the vendor. The contract price is usually lower than the price for labor, raw materials, and so on in the investor's home country but not as low as the costs of these inputs for a Romanian manager managing a domestic firm. This artificially low price is, however, a transfer payment from revenues derived from overpriced consumer goods.

The decree is silent as to methods to be employed in determining prices in the selected hard currency, but the Romanian authorities insist that everything is possible and negotiable. One of the most important parts in a contract for a joint venture in Romania is, therefore, negotiation for the domestic unit input and output prices.

The same principle applies to sales by the joint companies to domestic enterprises. The price will not be paid in lei by the buyer but will be reimbursed by the Romanian authorities in the selected hard currency on the basis of the negotiated output unit price.

Control Data Corporation (United States) negotiated a detailed package of wage rates and input costs; Falco (Italy), however, allocated roughly calculated global figures.

The concept of net income would be easy if the company's operations were exclusively domestic. Then, the company's net income would be uniquely determined by the difference in the output and input prices in terms of negotiated unit prices expressed in the selected hard currency. In this case, no part of the net income, denominated in hard currency, could be transferred abroad. It could be reinvested in the joint venture or in another association. However, the significant transactions of the joint venture will be international. In this case, prices paid for inputs and revenues received for outputs have very little bargaining latitude since they are determined exogenously by the international market. These transactions are recorded in the same hard currency unit as domestic transactions. The hard currency value in the accounts of any profit that results from purely international operations will be kept in a separate account. Another account will record the hard currency value made on purely domestic transactions. The hard currency account I, recording international operations, is divided in accordance with the equity between the domestic and foreign partners; after taxes, this share can be repatriated.

This method, in which the operations of the joint venture are divorced from the domestic price system in terms of price, is based on the official position of Romania. In COMECON meetings, Romania takes a strong stand against suggestions for setting up a price system within COMECON divorced from world market prices. While Romanian delegates accept the argument that the world market is subject to speculative trends and, therefore, that prices there too can be distorted, and while they also allow that the socialist systems create price stability over a specific period of time, they argue nevertheless that an "own price system" created within COMECON would be an artificial mechanism based on a formal mathematical pattern. Such a system, they argue, would be devoid of any economic content and would ignore the specific action of the Marxian "law of value" in economic relations. Therefore, the Romanian stand is that, while for domestic purposes a distorted price system is a must to achieve various objectives, the exchange of goods and international operations even among socialist countries cannot ignore objective laws and one cannot superimpose an artificial structure.

Since the joint venture is considered to be an international operation, it should not be subjected to the internal distorted price system but should mirror the relative scarcities representative of the world market. This position is the reason why joint ventures are virtually isolated from the domestic price structure and why managers should deal directly with Romanian authorities for domestic buying and selling on the basis of an agreed price system, close to the international price ratios.

Net profit is defined as what remains from net income after the subtraction of depreciation allowances, tax, and legally required reserves. Depreciation is dealt with in Article 27, which states that the rates of depreciation should, generally, be established in the contract of the association but that they may not be lower than the standard rates laid down by Romanian laws.

The legally required reserve fund amounts to 5 percent of annual profit and should be deducted from the annual profit. The deductions last until the reserve fund reaches 25 percent of the invested asset.

## Distribution of Profit

The net profit can be appropriated to form voluntary reserves; ploughed back to finance fresh investments; paid out to the shareholders as dividends, proportionate to their share; or any combination of the preceding.

The share of each appropriation may be determined by an enterprise policy formulated in the contract of the association or it can be determined by the general assembly of the shareholders. Concerning distribution of profit, the following can be expected:

1. In view of the legally required reserves, it looks unlikely that the shareholders will appropriate funds to form voluntary reserves.

2. The proportion of the profit ploughed back as investment will be the function of the planned rate of growth of the joint company. This can be decided by the assembly of the shareholders or laid down in the contract of the joint ventures. The hard currency is kept in two accounts, one generating from internal and the other from international operations. The proportion of the profit ploughed back should be divided again according to a ratio representing hard currency account I and account II.

3. As regards repatriation of dividends by the foreign partner, the situation is not totally clear. The likely situation is that the ability of repatriation of the annual dividend will be limited to the proportion of hard currency account II (that is, profit originating from international operations). In addition, the proportion of the foreign partner's equity enters the picture. For example, assume that the net profit is $100, which comes 40 percent from domestic operations and 60 percent from international operations. Further, suppose that the foreign partner's investment is 40 percent of total assets. Then, if no appropriations are made from hard currency account II to voluntary reserves or re-investments, the foreigner can repatriate 40 percent of the $60—or $24.

*Tax Holidays and Other Tax Incentives*

Tax holidays are regulated by the Council of Ministers of the Socialist Republic of Romania. A tax holiday may be granted at the end of the year in which taxable profits are generated. It may happen that the operation is profitable only in the last part of the year. Then, this part of the year and the proportionate part of the second year (to make the sum of one year) will be subject to a tax holiday. Thereafter, for the first two full calendar years, the rate of tax may be reduced to 15 percent.

If part of the profits are reinvested for a period of at least five years in the same joint venture or in other joint undertakings, then the tax due for that part of reinvested profit should be reduced by 20 percent; therefore, the reinvested profits should be taxed at a rate of 24 percent.

## The Effects of Tax on the Foreign Investor: An Economic Analysis

In 1971, a law on foreign trade was passed relating to joint ventures, which (1) guarantees foreign participants the right to transfer quotas of output, profit, and other amounts due them out of Romania, (2) calls for the establishment of bank accounts in Romania both in lei and in the currency of the foreign partner, (3) sets the rate of exchange for foreign currency at the noncommercial rate (which is 189 percent over the official rate), and (4) stipulates that the controlling body of such ventures include one or two members from the Ministry of Finance. In addition, this law establishes the tax rates that will apply to the profits earned by such joint ventures. Profits will be taxed at the rate of 30 percent, and there will be a surcharge of 10 percent on any dividends transferred out of Romania to Western stockholders. Interest income paid to foreign residents is subject to a 15 percent tax and royalties going to foreign residents are taxed at the rate of 20 percent. Nonresidents of Romania who earn technical service fees there will be liable to a 15 percent tax on such income. Foreign residents who are employed in Romania by a foreign corporation will be subject to Romanian taxes only if they remain in the country for longer than 183 days in a given year.

With this background, the question arises as to what will be the situation of the Western corporation participating in such a joint venture with the Romanian government as regards the taxation policies of Romania and the incidence of such taxes. The basic tax position of such a Western firm will not be altered greatly (if at all) because of the nature of the tax structure in its home country, which assesses a tax on all profits while allowing a credit for any tax paid to a foreign government if a tax treaty exists. Thus, assuming that deductible costs and depreciation allowances are similarly treated in Romania, the tax situation of a U.S. firm will not be that which would apply in the case of a firm that had previously operated in an environment free of profit tax. For this reason, many of the initial effects of such a corporate income tax will already have worked themselves out with regard to any single corporation and its position relative to other investment opportunities. However, because the goals of the Romanian planners may not coincide with those of the United States or other foreign stockholders (as carried out by the foreign managers of the firm), it is possible that the incidence of the corporate profit tax will be different for the foreign subsidiary than for its parent operating within the home country.

It has generally been held that such a profits tax will not alter a firm's output and pricing decisions because it does not affect the marginal cost or marginal revenue curves by which the firm makes its production decisions. This being the case, the whole of the tax, theoretically, will be paid from the profits earned by the firm being taxed. However, businessmen have continued to maintain that such a tax is part of operation costs, and they establish prices that will cover it. Just exactly what has been the actual case in the home country of the foreigner has not been determined, but the general consensus seems to be that at least a portion of the tax is shifted, either forward in the form of higher prices or backward in the form of lower wages paid to employees. Depending on which set of figures one examines, support can be gained for either the complete capitalization stance or for the complete shifting stance. Figures showing the average rates of return on invested capital demonstrate that such rates have not been shown to have an inverse relation to the tax rate level, as one would expect if the corporation bore the whole burden of the tax. On the other hand, before-tax profit as a percentage of total income originating in the corporate sector has not risen as one would expect it to do if the tax burden were being shifted. In addition, the fact that many other factors influence the movement of these figures serves further to obscure the incidence question.

The interesting situation of the Western firm participating in a joint venture with the Romanian government is that the two participants may very well have different goals regarding the operation of such a company. For the Romanians, the production and export of high-quality goods is of primary importance whereas, for the Western partner, the realization of some minimum level of profit can be assumed to be a primary goal. Thus, it seems likely that the incidence of the Romanian tax will be something other than that which prevails in the foreigner's home country.

The question of who is to bear the burden of a profits tax will be affected by the objectives sought by a firm. For the company seeking to maximize profits, the production decision will be one of equating marginal revenue with marginal cost, with production being expanded to the point at which the last unit produced bears a marginal cost just equal to the marginal revenue its sale brings to the firm. For the firm operating at the intersection of these two curves, the tax on profits will not cause any change of position simply because, even after payment of the tax, the firm's profit position is still at the maximum possible. As long as the tax rate is anything less than 100 percent, the marginal revenue earned by the last unit produced will still add a positive amount to after-tax profits.

In the case of a monopolist firm that has not been operating at its profit-maximizing position for one reason or another, it is possible that the imposition of the tax will cause it to move to such a position, thus raising its prices and shifting at least part of the tax burden on the consumers of its products. Also, in the case of oligopolistic firms, it is possible that they may see in the imposition of a profits tax the opportunity to raise their prices in concert without any one of them suffering a decline in sales. If the Western firm in the Romanian joint venture was one of a few large suppliers of a given product to the world market, the latter case would seem to be a likely outcome with the product prices of all the suppliers reflecting some portion of the profits tax paid by each of the firms.

Another possible situation would be that of the firm that seeks to maximize not its profits but its sales, consistent with earning some agreed-upon minimum level of profit. The firm in this case would avoid forward shifting of the tax because the resulting increase in price would serve to lower its sales volume (the two exceptions to this being mentioned above). The choice then would be for the firm to bear the whole burden of the tax out of its profits or to try to shift a portion of it backwards onto labor. Given the fact that the Romanian government is seeking primarily to enlarge its export total, sales maximization is, no doubt, its primary goal, its only concern with profits being that a sufficient level be achieved to induce the Western partner to remain in the venture. If the Western firm seeks the maximization of profits, it seems likely that unless the forward shifting can be accomplished without damaging the sales volume—that is, that it be done in concert with other producers—the Western partner will be constrained from such maximization.

Assuming that the Western and Romanian partners agree that shifting the burden of the tax forward will not serve their joint goals, there still remains the possibility that efforts will be made to shift a portion of it backwards onto the wage earners who are employed by the firm. In theory, short-run shifting will be unlikely if the firm has established its wage rates in accordance with the marginal revenue product since the tax will have no effect on the latter. In addition, as wages are inflexible downward, it would be difficult to make a direct shift of the burden backwards in the short run, although in the case of a firm entering the Romanian labor market, the rate of taxation will be known in advance and can thus be taken into consideration during the time of original wage rate determination. In addition, in the long run, the ability of the firm to pay for wage increases may very well be gauged by the amount of after-tax profit, in which case the firm would possibly be able to convince its workers that a small wage increase was all it could afford. In such a situation, the workers would bear a portion of the tax burden by virtue of the fact that they agreed to reduce their wage demands.

While this theory may apply more or less well to the situation of the large firm in the Western countries, where the work force is highly organized, it is not at all clear that such will be the case for the firm engaging in a joint venture in Romania. Firms in Yugoslavia have seen their wage bills increase at faster than normal rates. On the other hand, given the goals of the Romanian planners, the situation may be one of deciding to sacrifice workers' benefits in the hope of pacifying the Western partner. If such were the case, the Romanian workers would no doubt find themselves sharing the burden of the corporate income tax. (Given the fact that wage rates are very much lower in Romania than in the Western industrialized nations, it would seem that the U.S. participant would already have bettered his position simply by establishing the firm in Romania since the effect would be the same as if the parent company had been able to reduce materially the wage rates paid abroad. If, on the other hand, the rate of return on invested capital there turns out to be much higher than it is here, then the possibility suggests itself that the foreign partner may be more willing to bear the whole burden of the tax out of its earned profits.)

Another question that suggests itself in the matter of the incidence of the tax is the long-run effects it may have on the rate of investment. In a situation in which the corporation is unable to shift the tax burden, the rate of return to its stockholders must necessarily fall, resulting in a change in the position of the corporation relative to the other investment opportunities available to its stockholders. Such a lowered rate of return could not fail to have effects on the rate of investment that the firm is willing to undertake for the future. If the decrease in return is sufficient to discourage new investment, then, in the long run, the supply of products produced by the firm will fall, thus raising the price (assuming a constant or increasing level of demand). In this case, it may be that the tax burden will be borne by the corporation in the short run, only to be shifted to the consumers of its products in the long run. A similar situation would hold true for backward shifting since a reduced level of investment would mean lower demand for labor in the future and the accompanying fall in wage rates. In addition, if the assumption is made that corporations view the payment of dividends as more or less fixed costs, then the likelihood of the tax affecting future investment will be increased since the whole of the tax will have to be paid out of retained earnings. As this is one of the prime sources of internal investment financing for corporations, the result would surely be to lower the rate of future investment.

In the specific case of the joint venture firm in Romania, one of the requirements set by the Romanian government is that the firm establish a reserve fund by depositing 5 percent of each year's profit until the fund reaches the level of 25 percent of invested capital. This fund is also taken into consideration in determining the taxable profit of the firm. In this way, the Romanian planners seem to be seeking to offset the negative investment effects of the profits tax. This regulation, coupled with the reduced tax rate on reinvested profits, may offer sufficient incentive to the firm to forestall any curtailment of future investment.

All things considered, it seems likely that the Western firm participating in a joint venture with the Romanian government will find itself in a position that works against the forward shifting of the profits tax but is more conducive to its backward shifting. However, even should the firm find itself bearing the total burden of the tax, this does not necessarily mean that such a firm will find that its operations within Romania are not advantageous. Given the tax structure of the Western nations and their practice of taxing those profits that are remitted by a subsidiary back to the parent firm in the form of dividends, the question is mainly one of which government will get the tax revenue. Even though Romania's tax rate on profits is lower than that in most of the Western countries, the balance must be paid, minus any tax paid to Romania, when the profits are returned to this country. However, the fact that capital gains are subject to a lower rate than are profits suggests the possibility that the wise course for such a participating firm would be to pay out only such level of dividends as is necessary to keep the stockholders satisfied, meanwhile retaining the lion's share of the profit for reinvestment. Such action would lower the tax bill to Romania and would also serve to increase the value of the company stock. Taxes on such gains would thus be deferred until they were realized through sale and even then would be subject to the lower rate of taxation.

It has also been suggested that in the case of subsidiary firms, much of the profit could be transferred to the parent company by means of the transactions that take place between them. This would serve to circumvent the Romanian surcharge on transferred dividends, but the resulting profit shown by the parent company would have to be declared for taxation in this country; thus, the only effect would be to give the tax revenue to the government of the foreigner rather than to that of Romania.

In summation, then, the situation with regard to joint ventures would seem to be that even with complete capitalization of the profits tax, the Western firm stands to gain over the long run through such dealings with the Romanian government. Assuming that the goals of the two participants are not mutually exclusive, both participants come out ahead—one through the increase in sales of exports to Western firms for hard currencies and the other through the long-term appreciation in the value of its holdings.

## Taxation on Nonresident and Foreign Nationals

A new Romanian decree, which became effective on January 1, 1974, stipulates that individuals or firms that do not have a residence in Romania also have to pay taxes on certain types of income. (Any individual spending less than 120 days a year in Romania is considered nonresident.)

A 15 percent withholding tax, deducted at source by the Romanian payer, is levied on interest on commercial credits extended to Romanian debtors; commission fees received from Romanian enterprises on commercial transactions; fees received by foreign firms for rendering technical assistance to Romanian enterprises or for training Romanian personnel in Romania or abroad; income from quality and quantity control services; earnings from expert appraisals, medical, scientific and technical consultations, and associated services; and air and maritime transport (applies only to nationals of countries that impose similar taxation on Romanian nationals).

A 20 percent withholding tax is deducted at source on royalties or lump-sum payments for the sale of patent or know-how licenses, trade marks, or similar property rights.

The Romanian Council of Ministers reserves the right to raise the tax rates for foreign firms or individuals whose own countries impose higher taxes on the similar earnings of Romanian companies or citizens abroad.

In situations where double-taxation agreements apply, the Romanian tax will be adjusted accordingly, or not imposed at all. The reaction to this taxation on the part of the nonresident foreigner is predictable. He will try to arrange the contract in terms of net royalties or interest payments. If this arrangement cannot be obtained, then the amount of the taxes will be shifted forward and added to the license or service fees before the final price is quoted. A regulation (Instruction no. 1507/1154 of January 15, 1972) on Taxation of Commercial Representatives Licensed to Operate in Romania lists in ten sections the Ministry of Finance instructions on this subject.

There are two ways for commercial representatives to be taxed: Those paid by commissions are taxed on a net income basis; for those not paid by commissions, the tax is computed on an imputation basis. The imputed income depends on the number of employees, and the imputed taxable income varies in accordance with that; it reaches the maximum "Type D" (more than eight employees), where the imputed taxable income is 800,000 lei.

## A Summary of the Romanian Taxation System

In Romania, the law of taxation, despite its increased role, was not subject to such a comprehensive reform as it was in other socialist countries. In Romania, the advocates of the two-channeled taxation system say that combination of the taxes of the enterprise and of the profits levy, which system has been in force in the past decades, is most in line with national economic policy and is best for centralizing a greater share of social net income and for the centrally directed distribution of this income. In Romania, as in all centrally planned countries, the most important part of the revenue flowing into the state budget comes from the turnover tax and from the payment of all or part of the enterprises' profits.

According to current Romanian financial science, the part of the enterprises' profits to be paid into the state budget does not qualify as a tax although the legal form of such levy is, in many respects, typical of taxes. The profits achieved according to plan serve to finance the credits extended to mechanization, to replenish enterprise funds, and to contribute to subsidies given by the state according to plan and to the central budget and the budgets of the local bodies.

Above-plan profits serve as smaller investments in the fields of social and cultural policy and as contributions to technical development, enterprise funds, temporary financial assistance funds, and individual bonuses. The profit quotas are determined on the basis of the total profits of the enterprise.

All enterprises and all other economic organizations must pay a social insurance charge, which is calculated on the basis of the actual wage bill. This, too, is a tax category; its extent, however, is different, primarily according to the character of the institution concerned.

In the Romanian economy, artisans' consumer cooperatives pay a progressive income tax assessed on the basis of their profits. The cooperative farms must pay an income tax only if they produce commodities of a nonagricultural character or sell commodities that they have purchased.

The population has to pay a comparatively small number of taxes. All incomes earned by Romanian or foreign citizens are subject to income tax unless the latter are exempt under an agreement precluding double taxation. One specialized form of income tax is the tax payable by persons carrying on intellectual activities individually. Furthermore, the members of the cooperative farms—inasmuch as they enjoy individual incomes—have to pay a tax, since no tax is imposed on the cooperative farms on the basis of their actual farming incomes. Finally, the taxation system includes a number of local taxes and dues.

# HUNGARY

## A Liberal and Open Centrally Planned System

Hungarian economic policy during the 1960s offered a very interesting testing ground. This period saw the emergence of new ideas arising from the remnants of the Stalinist directive mechanism and from old concepts of economic policy. These new ideas led the Hungarian economists to the elaboration of a new economic model—the so-called New Economic Mechanism (NEM), which went into operation in January 1968. The study of Hungarian economic policy in the 1960s shows how changes in economic mechanisms and policy concepts can be made in a market economy that is open, planned, and noncapitalist.

It is not easy to describe this transformation in brief. The main laws and the regulations for their application cover roughly 3,000 pages, and the technical and theoretical literature would fill a small library.

The years that have passed since the introduction of this new model cover too short a span for us to judge whether it is a success or failure. However, it is already clear that the NEM has been much more efficient than the directive model; and, even though some aspects of the reform have been de-emphasized its spirit remains.

Hungary aims to create an efficient economic model for a developed, open, democratic, socialist society. They claim that they were not concerned with ideas of convergence or dominance of the profit motive or with theories of consumer sovereignty, but, in fact, these are the new concepts incorporated. The Hungarian economic structure is based on the following principles:

1. In a relatively developed industrial society with an extensive domestic and international division of labor, the most efficient form of organization of economic activity is the market exchange system, regardless of the form of ownership.

2. Because the means of production are publicly owned, the operation of the market can be regulated in such a way as to eliminate those disturbances that occasionally disrupt economic processes in a private enterprise system.

3. The basic instrument and control for the socialist market economy is the macro-plan. The plan has the same economic aims and objectives as the government, and it indicates the instruments at the government's disposal. The

market and the price system provide signals for the planners, which warn them that investigations and interventions are necessary to guide the economy in the desired direction. Therefore, the plan acts as a correcting mechanism.

4. The success indicator for efficiency is the profit, a measure of success and an automatic regulator of income distribution.

5. Competition is necessary; indeed it is an indispensable part of the mechanism for adjusting to a market equilibrium.

6. Such an economy needs a relatively free price system. It cannot function properly without the automatic adjustment carried out in response to constant changes in relative prices.

7. Decision making should be decentralized. A limited number of macro-decisions should be made by central authorities, while micro-decisions taken by the economic units should aim to achieve the goals more efficiently.

Hungary stresses the concept of cooperation with Western enterprise. Industrial cooperation with the firms of the developed industrial nations is considered one of the most important aspects of economic development because, as stated, "We must find substitutes for imports at any price."

Analyzing the aspects of the Hungarian economic structure, one recognizes the influence of Yugoslav market socialism. In fact, the organization is similar to the Yugoslav-type system without the workers' self-managed firms, its free international movement of labor force, or its safeguards against a return to a rigid central planning. In Hungary citizens have many liberal permissions but very few constitutional rights.

The price the Hungarian policy makers had to pay for these improvements was an unwavering loyalty to the international interests of the Soviet Union. Thus, Hungary is politically one of the most faithful allies of the USSR; Romania, on the other hand, subordinates the economic well-being of her citizens while maintaining a strict centrally planned system in exchange for her relative political independence from the Soviet Union.

## Ownership

In 1970, Hungary announced the principle of partnership between foreign and local firms, foreign firms including enterprises from the Western industrialized nations. This concept was announced as a device to reduce the burden of imports, promote exports, and thus ease the balance-of-payments problem. The conditions were elaborated in October 1972. The Hungarian regulations are much simpler than the Yugoslav or Romanian decrees, which are complex legislative actions. In Hungary, a so-called law decree issued by the minister of finance elaborates the regulations. In this short decree, many issues are left open to make the regulations as flexible as possible.

Joint ventures in Hungary, with respect to ownership, have a simple solution. They normally take the form of joint stock or limited liability companies. The limits of the foreign equity participation are not spelled out in the decree, but it is normally limited to 49.9 percent, which restriction can be relaxed, especially if several Western firms would like to participate in the undertaking.

It is an interesting provision of the decree that the foreign partner may apply to the Hungarian National Bank for a guarantee to secure the right of its ownership against any damages that may result from direct or indirect acts of the Hungarian state or from the actions of the Hungarian counterpart. The joint venture contract should, however, include the details of such guarantee. This guarantee is deemed to be a strong safeguard to protect the equity of the foreign partner, which can be in tangibles and intangibles.

If the venture is in commercial or service activity, only the concurrence of the Ministry of Finance is needed for a contract called a memorandum of the association. If the venture holds industrial assets and engages in industrial production, the approval of the Council of Ministers is necessary. This regulation is a considerable departure from the practice in Yugoslavia and Romania, where local authorities seek primarily industrial joint ventures engaged in various sophisticated production processes and using forms of superior technology. In Hungary, while the joint companies cannot regularly be engaged in production, they may contract Hungarian enterprises for production, and, in this case, the regulations provide room for involvement in the production process as regards quality control.

## Taxation of Joint Ventures

### The Determination of Gross Income, Net Income, and Profits

Under section 31 of Law Decree no. 19 of 1970, the minister of finance, in agreement with the minister of foreign trade and the president of the National Bank of Hungary, promulgated Decree no. 28 of 1972, defining the financial conditions of the establishing, functioning, and terminating of joint ventures.

In accordance with Hungarian financial law, joint ventures are considered to be Hungarian enterprises; consequently, the rules and procedures governing their money circulation, order of accounting, formation of funds, definition of profits, and taxation are the same as those governing local enterprises when Decree no. 28 is not applicable. Some related questions—and this is of great importance to the foreign partner—may be regulated in the contract; if this contract is approved, then such matters cannot be challenged on the basis of a financial rule that may be applicable to the enterprise.

Distribution of income within the joint venture is a most important feature. Gross income is defined in Hungarian bookkeeping as the value of all goods and services sold in the internal and international operations. The *gross bookkeeping profit* (net income) is the difference between gross income and the aggregate of the fixed and variable costs of the joint venture.

The measure of profitability is often used in Hungary to establish the success of business enterprises. If gross income is Y and gross profits is S, then profitability P is measured by the following ratio:

$$P = S/Y \quad (1)$$

The rate of capital productivity (A) is determined by

$$A = S/K \quad (2)$$

in which K is the average of the total fixed and circulating capital employed during the period of measurement. The productivity of labor (V) is

$$V = S/W \quad (3)$$

in which W represents the sum of wages and salaries.

For Hungarian enterprises, the gross bookkeeping profit is increased by the increment of the wage fund, but the joint ventures are exempt from wage increment levies. The gross bookkeeping profit is diminished by the sums set aside for the risk fund. The rate of the contribution should be outlined in the contract of the association, and this fund should be increased until it equals 10 percent of the capital of the association. After deduction of the risk fund, the association may create a so-called employee's participation fund out of gross profits. However, the amount of this fund shall not exceed 15 percent of total wages and salaries.

The regulations do not prescribe any further mandatory formation of additional reserves or funds, and the remainder of the gross profits is the so-called profit-sharing funds, which stands for net profits subject to taxation. After the tax burdens are paid, this is divided in accordance with the proportion of the equity; the repatriation, if the foreign partner decides for this solution partially or totally, is tax free.

One should mention, however, that in the case of Hungarian firms the profit-sharing fund after taxes is often augmented from (1) grants from ministries such as contributions to low-cost meals provided for personnel, allowances granted to workers going through personal difficulties, and subsidies to cover expenditure on day nurseries and other child-care services; (2) premiums granted to enterprises that have achieved particularly impressive records; and (3) income from institutions that are financed out of the resources of the profit-sharing fund. On the subject of the contract with the Hungarian firm and authorities, the question of possible miscellaneous contributions to the profit-sharing fund from outside sources based on the principle of equal treatment should be raised.

There is, however, a more important item that the foreign investor ought to note. Domestic enterprises receive decisive incentives through preferences in profit taxes derived from export activities. These preferences extended to 158 enterprises in 1972, and they yielded a reduction of about 10 percent in the total profit taxes of the said enterprises. The computation of this preference is simple enough; it is 2.7 forints* per export dollar earned.[4]

Taxes on the joint venture are more strict in Hungary than in the other selected countries, and this has resulted in some criticism in the Hungarian economic literature.[5] It is argued that international experience shows that, in the course of economic development, price and monetary systems eliminate superfluous and noninducive tax burdens, moderating the effects of direct taxation. It is pointed out that Hungary's tax system is archaic since it hinders the increase in efficiency, incentives, and a flexible enterprise policy. This process can push the economy back to the previous price-fixing methods.

The authors especially criticize the taxation of joint ventures, which they consider high and unjustifiable, especially the jump of the taxes from 40 to 60 percent when the joint venture records a profit rate of over 20 percent. They disagree with the assumption of the Ministry of Finance that "starting off with low profits causes a strong interest."

The authors propose two guidelines for tax policies: (1) The system of taxation should not swell the cost of the efficient entrepreneur by reducing his profit margin to the minimum—that is, the rate of tax should not be progressive with the increments in profits, and (2) the tax should be levied in a neutral way,—that is, it should not increase prices or decrease the incomes derived from labor.

### Tax Holidays and Other Tax Incentives

The decree does not give any special provision for tax holidays but lists a few tax exemptions applicable to joint ventures. Association with foreign

---

*Multiple exchange rates for the Hungarian forints, as of 1976, (forint per United States dollar) are as follows:

Official (end of year): basic official rate—9.73; effective devisa rate—8.513; tourist and noncommercial rate—20.25; socialist currency trade rate—26.12; hard currency trade rate—41.70.

Black market (average of end of month): unlicensed transfers abroad—37.25.

The Hungarian multiple price and exchange system forms one of the obstacles to convertability which is often discussed but is not on the agenda.

Certain changes are, however, expected to ease currency and other regulations related to both outgoing and incoming tourism.

participation is exempted from progressive profit tax in proportion to fixed capital, which amounts to paying up the centralized portion of the depreciation allowance. This relief is understandable since not all the association's capital comes from local resources. The joint undertaking is exempt from wage increment levies.

This levy, mainly a regulating tool, applies to all Hungarian enterprises. It is imposed whenever the average wage level, or the overall volume of wages, increases over the previous year and the percentage rate of increase is in excess of the percentage increase in profits. Such a levy is charged against the so-called sharing fund (net profit) of domestic enterprises. Thus, the net profit of the joint ventures, also earmarked for individual incentives, is not burdened by the wage increment levy. The associations operating as joint enterprises are not liable to an automobile tax.

The said minor tax exemptions are complemented by another more important benefit. If the joint venture utilizes its taxed profits for reinvestments in order to increase the assets of the association, then the appropriate part of the profit taxes may be refunded upon a special application submitted to the Ministry of Finance. This formulation is vague, however, and it should be clarified in the contract.

Joint ventures in Hungary can probably expect better conditions for their international operations in the near future. Hungary has applied for General Agreement on Tariffs and Trade (GATT) membership, and this would involve a significant reduction of domestic tariffs.

With introduction of the value-added tax (VAT) system, indirect taxes on commodities included in the foreign trade turnover are generally reimbursed; as a result, these commodities are, for the most part, taxed only in the importer's country. This means that countries that use only consumption-type taxes and can reimburse them, have an advantage over those countries that apply direct taxes. However, if the exporting country uses the VAT system and the importers do not, the import commodity is not burdened by taxes at all, and the importers are in a poor competitive situation. In this case, the importer is forced to apply high tariffs or a discriminatory import tax.

This is the reason why the present Hungarian literature, in calculative and analytical works, discusses the effects of the reduction of the present tariff level and methods of applying monetary and taxation system solutions similar to those of the GATT members. In one study, the author calculated that it would be possible to reduce the tariff level of production materials by 10 to 16 percent and that the gross price of products used for final consumption or export could be reduced by 8 to 10 percent as a consequence of joining the VAT system.[6]

At present, Hungarian customs duties on imports from the United States vary from 1 percent for raw materials, to 10 to 40 percent for semifinished goods and 80 to 100 percent for machinery, finished products, and consumer goods.

## Profit Tax on the Foreign Investor

Section 9 of the decree deals with profit taxes and taxlike obligations on joint ventures. A tax is levied on the sharing fund. The sharing fund is defined as the gross bookkeeping profits diminished by depreciation and various-level deductions. The sharing fund, which can be considered as net profits, is taxed 40 percent or 60 percent—40 percent if the rate of profit (measured as the ratio of gross bookkeeping profit and the association's net assets) is 20 percent or less and 60 percent if the profit ratio is over 20 percent.

Additional taxlike obligations of the association include (1) social security and pension contributions (the association is burdened with 17 percent social security contribution on monthly total wages and salaries; another part is deducted from the salaries of the employees); (2) payroll tax (this tax is paid similarly on monthly total wages and salaries, and it is fixed at 8 percent; therefore, the total contribution on wages and salaries, the aggregate of the social security and pension contribution, and the payroll tax add up to 25 percent of the monthly wage bill); and (3) communal tax (Decree no. 28 of 1972 does not refer to this obligation, but it is payable under general tax regulations, Decree no. 31 of 1970 of the minister of finance. It is set at 6 percent).

In view of its commercial or servicing character, the joint venture does not seem to have any other tax burdens. It is possible, however, that a turnover tax may be charged to the association provided it sells directly to consumers or to retail trade. If the joint venture is noncommercial and nonservicing (and acts with the approval of the Council of Ministers), a so-called foreign trade tax is imposed on its foreign trade activities, based on Decree no. 62 of 1970 of the minister of finance. The joint venture is not exempt from this tax, but its rate is individually fixed by the minister of finance and should be included in the contract of the association.

In view of its function and internal financial system, the joint venture may, in practice, be subject to the above-listed terms only. All these are central taxes. In Hungary, in contrast to Yugoslavia, taxation is centralized and can be imposed only by the central state power. There is, however, a possibility that some problems of taxation will be solved by the principle of reciprocity. If the foreign investor's country applies local taxes against joint ventures with Hungarian participation, certain taxes or similar contributions to the budgets of local autonomies are possible.

## Avoidance of Double Taxation

According to Section 11 of Decree no. 28 of 1972 of the minister of finance, "while implementing international agreements on double taxation, the standpoint of the Minister of Finance is decisive in the question of reciprocity." This rule applies to agreements recognized as valid also by the foreign party and enacted in Hungary: with Austria (Act XL of 1925), Italy (Act XXIV of 1928), Sweden (Act XXV of 1937), the Netherlands (Act V of 1940), and Switzerland (Act VI of 1949). It would be desirable to enlarge the network of agreements by new ones, as such an action might provide an incentive for further associations, and to amend the existing ones in view of the changes in taxation systems following World War II. A new treaty with Austria is under discussion.

The foreign partner faces further taxes outside Hungary against the profits that are transferable abroad under Section 11 of Decree no. 28 of 1972 of the minister of finance. Practice should rely on the findings of comparative public finance and jurisprudence, because often tax types bearing identical names,— for example, local tax, direct tax, property tax—cover different contents in the laws of the various states. And, vice versa, when different names cover identical taxes, the substance and actual applications of the taxes must be examined.

It should be observed at this point that even in the absence of agreements for avoiding double taxation and of other government conventions, there are, in Hungary, prescriptions for tax levies based on reciprocity. There might also be cases of de facto reciprocity, which means that exemption or reduction can be granted even in the absence of agreement or statutory rule.

## Taxation of Foreign Employees

Hungarian and international tax laws affect not only foreign corporations but also their employees of foreign nationality. As it is, the personal incomes are even more strongly jeopardized by the "double taxation" owing to the simultaneous application of the territorial and the personal principle of fiscal sovereignty. According to Decrees 35 and 36 of 1971 of the minister of finance, a foreign national shall be exempt from income tax provided his exemption is guaranteed by a treaty (that is, not only an agreement for the avoidance of double taxation) or by reciprocity; the extent of exemption is determined by such agreement or such reciprocity.

In the absence of a treaty or reciprocity, Section 8 of Decree no. 28 of 1972 of the minister of finance—according to which "employees of foreign nationality of the association may transfer abroad 50 percent of any kind of their incomes paid by the association, in a currency stipulated in the memorandum of association"—should be interpreted so that the employee may transfer abroad 50 percent of all his or her income earned in Hungary after deduction of the taxes paid in forints. (Under Hungarian tax laws, income is not identical with the receipts—that is, the gross sum of earnings, but only with that part over which the earner can dispose freely after the deduction of the charges.)

Foreign incomes of foreign nationals are exempt from tax in Hungary. The association—as a Hungarian taxpayer—may employ foreign nationals either in labor contract or in another way. The emoluments paid to them will be taxable accordingly. Those working in labor employment do not pay income tax on their permanent earnings; they pay only a progressive pension contribution (between 3 and 10 percent). This is deducted every month by the association and paid to the tax office. Random intellectual employees not under permanent labor employment (such as translators, technical designers) pay an income tax under Decree no. 36 of 1971 of the minister of finance at a progressive rate of 6 to 60 percent; however, they enjoy benefits in the assessment of the taxable assets, since an allowance of 10 to 50 percent is admitted for overheads. This deductible income tax involves a further communal tax of 10 percent which has the character of surtax, as its basis is the income tax paid.

A similar situation will apply to foreign nationals who have entered a labor contract in Hungary as a principal job, if they take on an auxiliary or part-time employment with an association. In this case they shall pay income tax at the following rates: 10 percent—up to 2,000 forint wages; 12 percent—up to Ft. 3,000; 15 percent—above Ft. 3,000 plus the 10 percent surtax for communal tax, as mentioned above. Both full-time and part-time employees are entitled to the services and facilities of social security—for instance, health insurance based on the labor contract. Under Decree no. 35 of 1971 of the minister of finance, incomes deriving from employment not subject to superannuation (pension) contribution are taxable by a general income tax at a rate of 3 percent (occasional physical work is exempt). As to other sources of income, the taxable basis is established after the deduction of the documented, actual expenditure (costs, overheads), the rate being progressive from 6 to 75 percent. This category includes earnings on property interests (for example, emoluments received from corporations, dividends, and so on). Foreign nationals are also affected by the tax payable on passenger cars with foreign license plates; the rates have been modified as from 1973 under Decree no. 48 of 1972 of the minister of finance.

The effect of the new statutory rule on associations does not cover matters settled by international agreements. Thus, treaties may set exemptions from the said taxation system or prescribe other obligations. Fiscal sovereignty may be limited positively or negatively, in a broad range. However, any such provision should be in harmony with the economic policies of the partner states, which, ultimately, determine the development of international economic relations. Accordingly, in the taxation of the associations, it is not the fiscal aspect that will be dominant in Hungary either.

Ministry of Finance Decree 7/1977 amends in some important respects the regulations governing the operations of economic associations and joint enterprises set up with Western partners. Such enterprises can now undertake production work in addition to trade and service activities already permitted. The decree also effects several improvements in procedural rules; taxation and social insurance contributions are simplified and reduced, foreign employees are allowed to transfer part of their incomes abroad, profits due to the foreign partner can be remitted in foreign currency, and the Hungarian National Bank can, in certain circumstances, underwrite the Hungarian partner's obligations toward the foreign partner.

The purpose of this decree is obviously to render cooperative ventures with Hungarian enterprises more attractive to foreign firms. Difficulties and misgivings (mostly in the legal sphere) have had a restraining influence on foreign participants, and since 1972 only three joint enterprises have been set up.

The new decree, as is claimed, has swept away the complicated legal and economic rules and tries to convince potential foreign partners that Hungary is eager to set up large-scale joint production enterprises with them. Hungary's primary aim is to improve its production technology and hence its export capacity. It is hoped that the foreign partner will contribute a more advanced technology with capital, and will, as a trade-off, derive several benefits in exchange, including easier access to socialist markets and closer control over its technical know-how and patents than would be possible within the framework of a license deal.

Some of the obstacles, however, remain. First come the problems of wages and salaries. How will the Hungarian and foreign employees be remunerated? The decree does not go into details on this touchy subject. At the root of the difficulty lies the fact that a foreign employee is normally not prepared to work in an enterprise outside of his home country for lower wages than he is able to receive in his place of domicile. Yet conspicuously higher incomes than those enjoyed by Hungarian wage earners doing similar jobs can cause tension. To pay Hungarians working in joint enterprises more is no solution, since that merely creates another tension between them and their less fortunate compatriots employed elsewhere. Second, the problem arising of the difference between the Hungarian and foreign price systems complicates cooperation. Hungary, as all the Soviet-type countries, has a dual price system; production and consumption prices, due to various state subsidies and levies, develop along separate lines. Third, foreign firms are reluctant to adapt themselves to the rules of a centrally planned economy and are not sufficiently familiar with Hungary's economic targets and conditions.

Despite these remaining difficulties it is evident that the 7/1977 Decree is more liberal than its predecessor and means a step forward in Hungary's economic cooperation with Western partners. West German companies have shown interest in the new legislation that makes possible setting up joint production enterprises, and a double taxation agreement signed between Hungary and the Federal Republic of Germany will provide added incentive to cooperate. To improve financial relations with the United States the Hungarian National Bank opened a branch in New York in addition to similar facilities in Zurich, Paris, Frankfurt, and London. Vienna has housed a small Hungarian banking house, the Zentral Wechsel und Kredit Bank, for over 50 years.

Hungary is seeking the creation of joint venture enterprises primarily in the chemical and food industries.

## Summary of the Financial Operation of Joint Ventures in Hungary

Hungary has established relatively few joint ventures, and they concentrate on services, trade, or assembly of kits (for example, Hirbow, a joint venture between Hiradastechnika and Bowmar Canada Ltd., assembles calculator kits); therefore, the regulation of finances is still on an experimental basis. It is expected that more detailed regulations will follow the rather short basic decree in which many questions are not treated, such as the limitation of joint ventures with respect to the sectors of the national economy. Specific agreements, as informants claim, can be rather easily obtained for individual joint venture, and they should be incorporated in the contract.

The value of the joint enterprise, the circulating capital, the mode of settlement of financial results, the pricing of inputs and outputs from and for the local market follow the Hungarian system and are expressed in the units of the local currency, forints. Nevertheless, the raw or semifinished material coming from abroad or marketed in foreign countries is expressed in terms of a selected hard currency valued in international prices. The joint enterprise's operating costs, earning, debts, and claims are shown in the venture's balance sheet and calculated in local currency.

The proceeds from sales of goods and services must be deposited in the joint venture's account with the Hungarian National Bank. In accordance with the enterprise's needs, the bank exchanges the credit balance in this current account for national currency, if the national currency in the account is not enough to cover the expenses.

All details on tax liability that are not explicitly regulated in the decrees should be included in the contract on the founding of the joint venture. The hard currency of the joint enterprise should be recomputed to local currency at the exchange rate or exchange coefficient agreed upon by the representatives of the foreign company and the officials of the host country. This should be subject to readjustments, and disputes should be settled by arbitration before an international forum, such as the Chamber of Commerce in Zurich. Hungarians have always accepted the position of the International Chamber of Commerce on disagreements between the partners.

## BULGARIA

### Stressing Economic Cooperation with the Soviet Union

Bulgaria's aim is to bring her economy more and more in line with the Soviet pattern, and her state plans are formulated according to the philosophy of cooperation with the Soviet Union. The Soviet Union seems reluctant to allow on her soil joint ventures between domestic enterprises and Western corporations, and this stand is also taken by Bulgaria. Bulgaria's joint ventures are incorporated in the West, and generally their function is marketing.

Bulgaria's per capita GNP is the lowest among the European socialist nations, but it is growing fast. Yearly increases, measured in real terms, are around 9 percent and are greatest in the industrial sector. An area of disappointment for Bulgarian planners is agriculture. Labor shortages and out-of-date equipment in the agricultural sector are responsible for poor performance. This explains the interest of Bulgarian policy makers in technologically sophisticated Western agricultural machinery. Other interests are mainly telecommunications equipment, pharmaceuticals, nonelectric machinery, and mechanical appliances. Lately, Bulgaria has become interested in obtaining electronic, oil extraction, and ship-building equipment.

Bulgaria's free trade agreement with Finland, eliminating trade barriers between the two countries, is reportedly the first of its kind between a centrally planned and a price-directed economy. A barrier to U.S. and Bulgarian trade is Bulgaria's inability to receive U.S. government credits until an agreement has been reached on defaulted bonds issued by the Kingdom of Bulgaria and presently held by U.S. citizens.

The cooperation that interests Bulgaria is turnkey projects. It is envisaged that hard-currency shortages be solved by the following methods: (1) the Western firm supplies a tractor plant, for example, and turns it over to Bulgarian authorities; (2) the sale of the plant and equipment is backed by government-guaranteed Western credit; (3) the Western firm, under a long-term marketing agreement, purchases tractors, engines, or parts from the completed Bulgarian firm and pays in Western currency in an amount equal to the Western credit extended to pay for the plant, plus interest; and (4) the Western firm resells the products it received in hard-currency markets and uses the proceeds to discharge the hard-currency debt and to gain profits.

At the end of 1974, the Bulgarian government adopted new legislation on "economic, industrial and technical cooperation with foreign juridical and physical persons." This legislation does not permit direct Western equity investment in the Bulgarian economy, but it has established the conditions for Western companies wishing to invest in the Bulgarian economy. It is sometimes claimed that this legislation, in practical terms, allows Western corporations to draw benefits similar to those of the joint ventures.

## Regulations on Foreign Economic Cooperation

On June 12, 1974, the Bulgarian State Council issued a brief decree, no. 1196, on economic, production, and technological cooperation with foreign firms and individuals,[7] which specified that the Council of Ministers should issue detailed regulations on its implementation. These regulations have now been published.[8] They give a clearer idea of the range of joint activities envisaged within the framework of expanding economic relations. The decree begins by stating that "economic, production, and technological cooperation between Bulgarian economic organizations and foreign firms and individuals is being encouraged." To this end, "favorable planning, financial, credit, customs, and other conditions are being created," and fulfillment of the obligations assumed by Bulgarian enterprises is guaranteed.

Both the decree and the regulations state that cooperation is to be carried out on the basis of long-term contracts with foreign firms or individuals, the results of which should be "mutually advantageous." Such activities, according to the decree, may be carried out on Bulgarian or foreign soil. The regulations list the various kinds of cooperation envisaged:[9]

> Joint creation of new production facilities or reconstruction and modernization of existing ones on the basis of the latest technologies and scientific-technological achievements;
> Joint scientific research, design, etc.;
> Joint manufacture of finished or semifinished products and exchange of products and parts, documentation, licenses, know-how, technological assistance, etc.;
> Joint participation in supplying or building complete projects on the territory of the contracting countries and in other countries;
> Establishment of joint enterprises outside the territory of Bulgaria for production or other economic activity, etc.

Both the decree and the regulations state that a foreign firm or individual, by sending specialists, may participate in measures undertaken by a Bulgarian economic organization to increase labor productivity, improve organization of production, introduce new technologies, or sell its products on the international market. This provision is in line with the first and third types of cooperation listed above and reflects the demand that better use be made of foreign experience and know-how.

The most interesting question in connection with the decree on cooperation with foreign countries and the relevant regulations is whether or not Bulgaria will allow jointly owned enterprises to be set up on her territory. The answer would seem to be negative in light of the fifth type of joint enterprises to territories outside Bulgaria. The fact that the regulation governing this type of cooperation ends with "etc." could, however, imply that additional possibilities exist, including joint enterprises in Bulgaria. Moreover, the provision in the decree that joint activities may be carried out on either Bulgarian or foreign territory also seems to leave the possibility open. If this is so, it would obviously be allowed only in exceptional cases. It is well known that in recent years Bulgarian officials have repeatedly declared that mixed enterprises on Bulgarian soil are not acceptable. The keen interest manifested by Bulgaria in foreign know-how, technological assistance, and credits expressed during Deputy Premier Ivan Popov's 1974 visit to the United States may lead to exceptions to the general rule.

All contracts under the provisions of the decree and the regulations must be authorized from above before being signed. It is possible that special circumstances may be recognized through such advance approval if a joint venture of particular benefit to Bulgaria's economic development is involved.

Concerning payments among the contracting partners, both the decree and the regulations say that these should be made "entirely or partly" in goods or services connected with the contract, or with funds resulting from the fulfillment of the contract. In addition, the regulations contain special provisions concerning the monetary involvement of the foreign partners and aimed at relaxing certain restrictions. A foreign firm or person "may receive part of the economic effect achieved through cooperation" if one or a number of specific conditions are met—for example, if the cooperation has led to the speedy adoption of new, efficient technology, if the foreign partner has financed the whole or the major part of a project, and so on. Participation in the economic effect may also be authorized under conditions other than those listed.

The regulations also contain a provision allowing foreign specialists who work in Bulgaria in fulfillment of a cooperative contract to transfer abroad, through the Bulgarian Foreign Trade Bank, up to 50 percent of their remuneration. The labor and social conditions applicable to such specialists are to be settled by the contract.

As can be seen from the above, the regulations do not contain any particularly liberal provisions, but they do provide a basis for increased economic cooperation with foreign firms, in which Bulgaria is strongly interested. Whether such cooperation will be attractive to foreign partners and will really expand will depend to a large extent on the individual contracts and on the kind of authorization given for each of them.

## Personal Income Tax Rates and Tax on Profits of Corporations

*Darzhaven Vestnik,* no. 53, July 6, 1973, published the texts of several articles of the law on income tax as they had been amended by a recent session of the National Assembly. The amendments included new tables of tax rates to be applied to income from wages and salaries; to income from fees paid to artists, scientists, engineers, and technicians; and to income from "private activities." The new provisions replaced four tables, some of which were as old as the law itself (1950) and were all in effect by January 1, 1974.

The new table on tax rates for income from wages and salaries (Article 4) provides complete exemption from income tax for monthly earnings up to 80 leva* (formerly, monthly incomes of, for example, 61 and 79 leva were taxed, respectively, 2.98 and 5.04 leva). It should be noted, however, that 80 leva is now the minimum monthly wage in accordance with the decision of the December 1972 plenum and a decree of March 9, 1973, so the new exemption limit is meaningless in virtually all cases.

The 1966 tables provided varying tax rates for monthly incomes up to 72 leva and a single basis of calculation for incomes exceeding this sum (4.08 leva plus 12 percent of the part of the income above 72 leva). In the new tables, however, varying rates are envisaged for seven different income brackets, ranging from 80.01 leva to incomes exceeding 340 leva. The new rates mean reductions of tax in the lower brackets and small upward or downward changes for higher incomes, as Table 4.6 shows.

The considerable reductions in tax on low incomes is a first step toward the gradual abolition of all income taxes imposed on wages and salaries (which was announced by the December 1972 plenum), but there is still a long way to go.

No changes were made in the tax table for income received by scientific and artistic workers, writers, and so on, stemming from activities outside their regular employment (Article 8), as far as small and medium-size incomes are concerned. The new table differs from the old one, however, inasmuch as it

## TABLE 4.6

### 1966 and 1973 Tax Rates

| Monthly Income | Existing Tax | New Tax |
|---:|---:|---:|
| 90 | 6.24 | 3.00 |
| 100 | 7.44 | 7.00 |
| 105 | 8.04 | 7.60 |
| 120 | 9.84 | 9.40 |
| 160 | 14.64 | 14.20 |
| 260 | 26.64 | 26.90 |

*Source:* Compiled by the author.

---

*Currency units (leva per U.S. dollar) as of 1976 are as follows: Official (end of month)—.97; black market—2.51.

provides six differentiated rates for annual incomes exceeding 1,500 leva and going up to 40,000 leva and above; until 1974, there had been a single rate for all such incomes above 1,500 leva. The new rates mean a large progressive increase in taxation on high incomes of this kind. For instance, an artist who earns 12,000 leva a year from such sources used to pay a tax of 1,781.80 leva; now he is charged 3,221.80 leva; on an annual income of 30,000 leva, the old tax works out at 5,011.80 and the new at 7,471.80 leva.

In the tax rates applicable to fees earned by engineers and technicians outside their regular employment (Article 10), the new table provides for a reduction of tax on the lowest earnings and differentiated rates for higher incomes—again, as in the new table for artists, with increases for the highest earnings.

In the new table on taxation of income from private activities, notably that of private artisans, the tax rates were partly raised beyond the very high level that was set in 1950 and increased in 1968. There is no nontaxable income in this category, and the lowest rate (9 percent) now applicable to annual incomes of up to 500 leva will apply only to those of less than 200 leva. The new rates mean that for an income of 400 leva the tax will be 42 instead of 36 leva, and for an income of 500 leva, the tax was raised slightly, and there are similar differences for higher incomes.

The increases in this category of tax rates may seem surprisingly small in view of the fact that, when speaking of the abolition of income tax on wages and salaries at the December 1972 plenum, Finance Minister Todor Zhivkov called for a new scale of taxation on incomes from the private sector, which "must be progressive enough to prevent the earning of larger incomes than those earned by the corresponding categories of workers in the social sector." This was carried out in regard to free-lance work by artists and technicians, but not in the case of private artisans. It should not be forgotten, however, that the tax rates applicable to these categories were already very high and that many steps have been taken in the last few years to reduce the activities of private artisans to a minimum.

Corporations, including foreign associations, are not subject to corporate income tax, and profits are not burdened by a tax levy.

## The Bulgarian Joint Venture

Bulgarian joint ventures are operating in several Western industrialized nations, including Italy, West Germany, Austria, and France. Such cooperation with capitalist countries is common in other COMECON countries, the USSR, Poland, the German Democratic Republic, Hungary, Romania, and Czechoslovakia all having similar ties with Western countries.

Contracts for joint ventures with Bulgarian firms are established through the foreign trade organizations. The creation of joint ventures on foreign soil places Bulgarian exports on the capitalist markets and channels Western products back to Bulgaria. Bulgaria's use of the normal channels for exporting to the industrialized West has not been very successful, mostly because her use of the foreign trade organizations, different middle men, foreign trading agents, and so on, has lacked sophistication. With the joint venture, it is possible to exclude the middle man since direct contacts are provided for selling goods abroad.

It can be said that the Bulgarian joint venture on foreign soil serves one main goal: "the elimination of foreign middlemen and representatives of Bulgarian enterprise, and the creation of opportunities to utilize both the advantages of importing and exporting as well as the profit from wholesale and retail trade."[10]

## A Bulgarian Representative of Foreign Firms: INTERPRED

Bulgaria seems eager to assist those foreign companies that wish to establish commercial and business relationships with their Bulgarian counterparts outside Bulgarian soil. On the basis of Decree no. 289 of the Committee for Economic Coordination of July 3, 1970, an association was established under the name of INTERPRED for facilitating the activites of foreign companies. INTERRPRED acts as a commercial agency and supplies valuable information to foreign businessmen who wish to develop economic relationships between their own and Bulgarian business organizations.

INTERPRED's governing body, the Council of the Association, passed a decision by which other bureaus or representations can be admitted to membership in the association. INTERPRED is a separate juridical person with headquarters in Sofia. It carries out its activity on the basis of an independent bank account and is not financed by the state. At present, it comprises 12 bureaus, which concentrate on groups of countries, each bureau responsible for a separate group of noncompeting foreign businesses; in this manner, manufacturing and commercial secrets are safeguarded.

The statute of the association was accepted by the Council of the Association in its session of October 31, 1970 and was approved by the minister of foreign trade. Section II, paragraph 7, of the statute sets forth that the bureaus shall independently conclude agreements for commercial representation and shall act as intermediaries for foreign companies in connection with the aims and activities of the latter. INTERPRED puts these companies in touch with the proper Bulgarian officials and the foreign trade organizations, gives them legal advice, organizes symposiums and consultative meetings, and aids foreign companies with their participation in the annual International Plovdiv Fair.

## A Summary of the Operations of Joint Ventures and Their Taxation in Bulgaria

Bulgarian joint ventures operate only on the soil of foreign countries, and their purpose is to help Bulgarian firms export their products. Bulgaria is also interested in various forms of economic cooperation with Western firms on her soil—namely, turnkey projects for which she usually compensates the Western firm with actual produce or with productive capacity.

Ukaz no. 85 of August 31, 1974, by virtue of an unfinished sentence, seems to allow that provision might be made in the future for establishment of joint ventures on Bulgarian soil, but this seems unlikely until the time that such ventures are established in the USSR. The Bulgarian economy follows Soviet policy closely, and one cannot expect Bulgarian policy makers to imitate the Romanian or Hungarian patterns.

With respect to corporation income, Bulgarian taxes follow the Soviet model strictly, and no taxes are levied at present on the income of foreign enterprise operating cooperatively in Bulgaria. Foreign personnel in Bulgaria are subject to the same income taxes as Bulgarians; they can repatriate 50 percent of their earnings from Bulgarian operations. There is, however, a hidden taxation originating from the overpricing of consumer goods, but this burden hits everybody. Foreigners are exempt from the almost compulsory purchase of government bonds, which represents another heavy tax burden on the local population. Workers are expected to subscribe to bonds, which are deducted from their monthly salary. When these are repaid, it is time to buy a new series of bonds. Thus, the original investments are, in fact, never paid back; instead they increase in proportion to the income.

Profit taxes are not levied on corporations or on cooperative projects.

## CZECHOSLOVAKIA

### Czechoslovakia: "Classic" Soviet-Type Model

Before the August 1968 invasion of Czechoslovakia by the Soviet Union, the policy of the Czechoslovak government, as described by the economic architect of the Prague Spring, was

> to take advantage of offers to cooperate with Western firms in order to modernize plants and to introduce new and more effective production and, in addition, with the help of the Western partner, to penetrate markets that our country has abandoned on its own accord or that have been closed to us over the past twenty years.[11]

After the Soviet invasion, the goal of the country can be summarized as the "full restoration of the socialist character of the society and economy."

This means, as recent symposiums have demonstrated[12] that the key problem is the question of socialist ownership and its defense "against bourgeois ideologists and revisionists."

In this atmosphere, complicated by other international problems such as the question of Czechoslovak gold reserves held by the United States, it is totally unlikely that joint ventures in Czechoslovakia can be established with Western firms. In spite of the fact that official data on the Czechoslovak economy are on the whole favorable, the country has a serious handicap that has existed for a number of years and that the finance minister calls "our Achilles heel." This is investment.[13]

Since 1972, rising material costs, a low shift-coefficient of the industry, a high rate of absenteeism, growing stockpiles (attributable to difficulties in selling technologically obsolete products), and especially chronic deficiencies in the investment sector have been commonplace. The Soviet-type model requires extensive investments in the production sphere at the cost of the nonproduction sectors; this can be the source of economic imbalance and inflationary pressures. On October 25, 1972, the Czechoslovak government discussed this question and decided to reduce the number of new constructions.[14]

Czechoslovakia is deeply in need of economic cooperation with Western countries to achieve the goals listed by Ota Sik. On November 10, 1972, a new Law on Procedures for the Concluding of Agreements on Economic Cooperation with Countries Abroad was promulgated.[15]

However, in spite of its promising title, it seems designed to restrict cooperation with the West and favors autarky in the field of technological development.

## Regulations on Foreign Economic Cooperation

The above Law no. 85 came into force on January 1, 1973, and abrogated a notice issued by the Ministry of Foreign Trade on August 14, 1968, on Conduct of Industrial Cooperation with Foreign Firms. This notice was discussed in the supplement to *Hospodarske Noviny* (July 26, 1968):

> Negotiations on cooperation fall into the sphere of enterprise activities. The higher economic agencies, including the ministries concerned, only express an opinion from the aspect of concept and coordination. . . . The agreement will be signed by the Czechoslovak production firm provided that consent of the banking system has been obtained. . . . In the banking sphere, consent for the financing of cooperation will be withheld if the Ministry of Foreign Trade has raised objections from the point of view of trade policy. . . .

The notice was issued 14 days before the August 1968 invasion, in a political and economic situation that was completely different from that prevailing today. Therefore, it is hardly surprising that the new law reversed the procedures involved in judging the expediency of cooperation.

An organization that wishes to establish cooperation with a firm abroad is now obligated to apply to the Ministry of Foreign Trade for its consent. This requirement ensures that the interests of the national republics—Czech or Slovak—will not be decisive in establishing cooperation.

The ministry will examine whether the proposed cooperative undertaking is in harmony with Czechoslovak economic and foreign policy. The authorities are required to consider the effect that the proposed venture will have on existing economic relations with foreign countries and on the international obligations binding on Czechoslovakia. No doubt what is meant here are bilateral relations and obligations in regard to the USSR and other countries of the socialist bloc and also agreements made within the framework of COMECON.

If the proposal is approved by the Ministry of Foreign Trade, it will be checked by the Czech or Slovak ministry that supervises the organization wishing to establish cooperation to determine whether the undertaking is in the interest of the respective national republic.

Cooperation always has a foreign-exchange aspect; thus, the Czechoslovak State Bank, which implements foreign exchange policy, must examine the proposal after the two ministries have approved it.

The 1972 law favors autarky in the field of technological development. This is indicated as well in the law on inventions (no. 84/1972), which reserves to Czechoslovakia the inventions of Czechoslovak citizens whether they live on Czechoslovak soil or not.

## The System of Taxation in Czechoslovakia

Czechoslovakia's monetary policy was formed after World War II under economic conditions unlike those in the neighboring socialist countries. That is, under German occupation, Czechoslovakia had been forced to adopt, among other economic measures, the German system of taxation. The fundamental transformation of civil financial law was begun in the period of the First Five-Year Plan (1948–53). With the advance of nationalization and collectivization, the two-channel tax system was established by which the enterprises paid turnover tax and various "yield withdrawals." During 1953–60, there was no significant change in the Czechoslovak tax system, but during 1966–69 significant reforms were introduced: financial incentives to enterprises, increasing enterprise autonomy, and coordination of enterprise and national economic interests.

A law passed in 1966 formed the basis for the Fourth Five-Year Plan and determined the basis for enterprise taxation in gross income and profits. This meant a decisive change. Since October 1971, state enterprises have paid five types of contribution to the central budget: payment on profits (75 percent of the net profits according to the balance), a contribution on tied-down fixed assets (5 percent of the value of buildings, machinery, and installations, or 2 percent for mining industry and gas-supplying enterprises), a tax on surplus wages (paid by those enterprises in which per capita average wages have increased in comparison with the previous year, on the basis of a progressive index on the full sum of the gross wages), a social insurance contribution (25 percent of the wage fund), and amortization (this includes the supplementary payments required as a result of misdemeanors).

In Czechoslovakia, an independent agricultural tax has existed since 1948. It includes the land tax and the tax on agricultural income. In addition, there is a payment on agricultural property, which is placed in the republic's state funds that are established for increasing the soil's fertility.

The elements of tax system for the population are as follows. Tax on incomes derived from private activities and the use of property range from 5 to 65 percent if they do not fall under the income tax law. There is an income tax on incomes derived from wages and salaries. The tax on an earner who supports two persons ranges from 5 to 20 percent. Cooperative farm members must pay an agricultural tax on vineyards or tobacco within the private plot, or on specialized animal husbandry. Old age allowances over 700 crowns monthly are in a special income tax category. Rented flats and cars are also taxed. Among the socialist countries, the Czechoslovak system of taxation is the most highly complex and the fullest in scope.

## Summary of Western Cooperation with Czechoslovakia

In spite of some optimistic reports coming from the U.S. Department of Commerce, Domestic and International Business Administration, doing business with Czechoslovakia is extremely difficult for Western firms. Although relations with the industrialized countries and even the problems of joint ventures are occasionally discussed in Czechoslovakia[16] the view of the present author is that Czechoslovakia will be the last country in the Soviet bloc to permit joint ventures on her soil.

The reasons for this are mainly political. Czechoslovak leaders are eager to prove that their country is not "Western-oriented"; they are sensitive to such criticism since, among the European socialist states, Czechoslovakia has the most sophisticated labor force, the most developed economy, and the most internationally oriented population (the German Democratic Republic notwithstanding). Before World War II, Czechoslovakia was a relatively liberal state but now it seems unable to give its economy even the limited degree of freedom usual in some other communist states.

As is evident from the foregoing, taxation of Western enterprise cannot be examined for the case of Czechoslovakia since Western enterprise, in equity form, does not exist on Czechoslovak soil.

What the Czechoslovaks now seek is such cooperation agreements with Western countries and in Latin America with Brazil as can guarantee long-term benefits to the Czechoslovak economy while guaranteeing greater outlets for Czechoslovak products to Western and Latin American markets under compensatory payment agreements.

However, the political atmosphere in Czechoslovakia is chilly and the prospects of any relaxation of the highly restrictive methods that the Ministries in both Prague and Bratislava continue to apply still seem remote.

## NOTES

1. See *Ekonomska Politika,* Belgrade, 12 August 1975; *Statisticki Godsnjak Jugoslavie* 1973 *(Statistical Yearbook of Yugoslavia)* (Belgrade, 1973); *Information on Investments of Foreign Partners in Yugoslav Enterprises—Joint Ventures* (Belgrade: Yugoslav Investment Bank, 1971).

2. See A Law on Income Tax of the Organizations of Associated Work, *Official Monitor* of the S.R. of Serbia, no. 4/73, p. 83; *Official Gazette* of the S.R. Bosnia-Herzegovina, no. 36/72, p. 1057.

3. See *Scinteia,* December 31, 1974; *Romania Libera,* December 29, 1974; *Commerce Today,* July 23, 1974.

4. I. Orszagh, "Analysis of the Operation of the Profit Tax Preferential Export Incentive System," *Kulgazdasag* 17, 11 (1973):813–24.

5. L. Racz and F. Vissi, "Direct Taxation of Profits or Alternative Solutions?" *Kozgazdasagi Szemle* (Economic Review) 20 (1973):1060–74.

6. L. Koczka, "The Hungarian Tariff Level and Taxation System," *Penzugyi Szemle* (Financial Review) 18, 11 (1974):943–50.

7. *Darzhaven Vestnik* no. 46, June 14, 1974.

8. Ibid., no. 73, September 20, 1974.

9. Ibid.

10. "Regulations Governing Foreign Firms with Bulgarian Participation," *Durzhaven Vestnik,* no. 13, 1969.

11. Ota Sik, *Czechoslovakia: The Bureaucratic Economy* (White Plains, N.Y.: International Arts and Sciences Press, 1972), p. 107.

12. Symposium on Socialist Ownership, Prague, October 17, 1974.

13. Rudolf Rohlicek, "The Investment Sector: Our Achilles Heel," *Pravda* (Bratislava), May 4, 1973.

14. "Comprehensive Analysis of the State of Investments and Measures to Improve Management and Planning," *Planovane Hospodarstvi,* no. 5, 1972.

15. No. 85/1972, published in *Sbirka Zakonu.*

16. "Economic Cooperation is of Great Interest to Our Economy," *Hospodarske Noviny* (Economic Weekly), October 15, 1974.

CHAPTER

# 5

## CONCLUSIONS AND POSTSCRIPT

## CONCLUSIONS

The foregoing background illustrates that in the group of the European countries calling themselves "socialist," only Yugoslavia, Romania, and Hungary have issued legislation or decrees to allow equity-style joint business ventures with Western companies on their soil. The remainder of the European socialist states, which with the exception of Albania are part of the Soviet bloc, follow the example of the USSR, which does not recognize Western capital investments in her economy. However, it would be the most elementary mistake to lump Yugoslavia together with Romania and Hungary on the grounds that they all seem eager to have Western capital investment in the form of joint stock companies for the achievement of various economic goals.

Yugoslavia, as it has been stated, is not a centrally planned economy; therefore, it should be treated separately. It is the only one of our selected communist countries where soviets—that is, workers' councils—have power. Paradoxically, the soviets were abolished in the Soviet Union, and they were never given power in the other Soviet-type economic systems. Yugoslavia's economy is a decentralized market socialism where the most important success indicator is the profit of the enterprise.

Further, Romania and Hungary should not be separated from the other centrally planned economies on the superficial grounds that they are ready to cooperate with Western enterprise in joint ventures in their home countries.

The strong common denominator in the centrally planned economies is that taxation, especially in its hidden excise tax form, is the most prominent feature of economic life. In the command economies of the Soviet bloc, the accepted policy is a forced industrialization process, and the average rate of taxation with compulsory government bonds on the citizen is probably the highest in the world. Western investors must realize that, in centrally planned systems, prices in the state sector are purely formal in character. In this segment of the economy, the monopolistic producer and the monopsonist buyer are the same, and prices are considered only devices to trace the movements of funds allocated to further production. For this reason, the planner relies primarily on administrative orders in physical terms to achieve his objectives: economic growth and speedy industrialization. Within the state sector the market plays only a vestigial role.

A mature centrally planned economy, nevertheless, makes considerable use of the market in the guidance of economic activity between the state and the private cooperative sector. In this stage, the planner (although he has the power to do otherwise) refrains from requisitioning and/or using other crude methods of coercion to distribute or redistribute the product mix in accordance with various national goals. Instead, the command economy relies on a careful manipulation of the price and tax structure, taking into account various economic factors such as the aggregate demand and supply coming from the private cooperative sector.

These characteristics lead to an important practical conclusion for the joint venture that has not often been discussed. In the centrally planned economies of Romania and Hungary (as well as in the other Soviet-bloc countries), the prices of goods allocated to the state sector are biased downwards and the value of commodities aimed for the private cooperative sector are biased upwards. Therefore, for the internal operation of the joint business venture, a separate price system should be established that reflects the relative prices prevalent in the world market and is independent of the internal distorted price structure. In the Romanian regulations concerning joint ventures, this proviso is included; in Hungarian venture agreements it is not clear how the internal price biases will be dealt with.

A side effect of the upward consumer price distortion is that foreign employees associated with joint ventures, when they rely on the supply of domestic consumer goods, will have to pay hidden excise taxes, which can be extremely high in centrally planned systems. This punitive tax on consumption goods ought to be considered as an unavoidable business expenditure. Therefore, it should be deductible from the employees' personal income tax in their home countries. Foreign employees may also be subjected to artificially high official exchange rates to purchase unconvertible domestic currency. Similarly, the difference between the official and the unlicensed free market exchange rate creates a business loss and, therefore, these losses created by the excess rate of exchange ought to be similarly tax deductible.

The following scheme is proposed to sum up the regulations related directly or indirectly to taxation:

*Accounting Procedures*
1. Yugoslavia

(a) Joint ventures in Yugoslavia are based on the concept of "free contractual regulations"; therefore, all accounting rules should be included in the contract.

(b) The Yugoslav partner is required to maintain separate accounts.

(c) The calendar year is taken as the time unit reflected in the balance sheet.

2. Romania

(a) The accounting system should be outlined in the contract.

(b) Romanian personnel are paid in domestic currency, and this should be purchased on the basis of a separately determined exchange rate from the Romanian National Bank.

(c) All hard currency payments of the joint business venture must be generated from funds of the business venture or financed by loans coming from abroad.

3. Hungary

(a) The accounting system should be outlined in the contract and approved by the Ministry of Finance.

(b) A "risk fund" should be set aside in accordance with the contract of the joint venture; annual losses can be charged against this fund.

(c) Operations that use foreign currencies and raise credits are guided by the same rules as domestic organizations.

(d) Wages and contracts with local personnel should be in accordance with Hungarian statutory rules and approved by the Ministry of Finance.

*Business Taxes*
1. Yugoslavia

(a) The domestic partner is obligated to pay the tax and the foreign investor should provide his share, which is, on the average, 35 percent of profits.

(b) If from the profits 25 percent is reinvested, the tax rate decreases to 29.75 percent, and it decreases progressively more with higher rates of reinvestmnt.

(c) There is a considerable variation in the rate of taxation; in the undeveloped parts of the country the rates are considerably lower.

(d) If the Western partner keeps at least 20 percent of his profit in a local bank, he may be exempted from tax on interest earned on these deposits.

(e) Royalty income is taxed at graduated rates of 10–25 percent on net royalties.

(f) Personal-service income taxes on foreigners may be as high as 70 percent on incomes generated by rendering services in Yugoslavia.

2. Romania

(a) Romania taxes the joint venture's annual profits at a rate of 30 percent.

(b) An additional 10 percent withholding tax is levied on distributions to nonresidents—that is, transfers abroad; therefore, the total taxes amount to 37 percent.

(c) If profits are reinvested for a period of five years, then profit taxes are reduced from 30 to 24 percent.

(d) Tax exemptions may be granted from the Council of Ministers for the first year and tax reductions (up to 50 percent) for the following two years.

(e) Romania's regular tax rate is applied to royalty income. The tax on this type of income is 20 percent and is also applied to receipts for marketing know-how and patents. Cultural royalties are subjected to a 15 percent tax levy.

3. Hungary

(a) Profit taxes are progressive: 40 percent and 60 percent. The rate of 40 percent should be paid if the association records profits up 20 percent; 60 percent if the profit on the net assets is over the 20 percent limit.

(b) If profits are reinvested, the taxes on those profits are reimbursed.

(c) The joint business venture does not pay taxes on wage increases, on the centralized portion of depreciation allowances, or on fixed assets, as domestic corporations do.

(d) Pension contributions and social security payments are the same as for domestic firms.

(e) International tax questions are judged on the basis of reciprocity in the absence of tax treaties.

*Transfers*

1. Yugoslavia

(a) The foreign partner is free to transfer his share of net profits abroad, provided that the enterprise has the foreign exchange at its disposal.

(b) The foreign partner is permitted, under some circumstances, to withdraw his investment, or part of it.

(c) The source for foreign currency for repatriation is the retention quota, which is 20 percent of export proceeds for all industries and 45 percent of revenues generated from tourism. In addition, an allowance of convertible currency allocated to joint ventures amounts to 33 percent of the exports. For remittance of investment, these sources are amended by an annual allowance of 5 percent on the depreciation.

2. Romania

(a) The foreign partner is free to transfer his share of net profits abroad from the enterprise foreign exchange fund.

(b) Such transferred profits are subjected to an additional 10 percent dividend withholding tax.

(c) The portion of the profit that goes to the reserve fund cannot be transferred abroad.

3. Hungary

(a) Net profits are transferable, and capital repatriation in convertible currency, after payment of taxes, is secured.

(b) The foreign partner can withdraw tax-free his share of the association in accordance with the rules stipulated in the contract of the association.

(c) Foreign personnel is limited to transferring abroad 50 percent of wages or salaries.

After the foreign investor pays his share of taxes in the host country, he is, naturally, usually subject to "unlimited tax liability" on the repatriated profits in his home country. If the foreign share of the joint venture has financial, economic, and organizational ties with a parent company, then, in most Western countries, the foreign share of the equity investment in the socialist countries is regarded as a subsidiary. Repatriated profits, together with the capitalization of know-how, are subject to additional corporate income tax in the home country of the foreign investor. In most cases, various provisions can provide tax relief, and law provides for foreign tax credit. In some special cases, however, it is extremely difficult to eliminate tax hardships, and neither international tax-treaty law nor the model agreement of the Organization for Economic Cooperation and Development (OECD) offers a solution to this problem. Table 5.1 lists the corporate tax rates of Western countries and thus shows differences similar to those found among the socialist states.

Considering the various direct and indirect burdens on the net profits of the Western equity in joint business ventures, one may assume that the direct returns will not be high. This proposition cannot be tested, however, against actual data since it is still too early to compare figures on a larger scale.

One can also argue that even small repatriations could be considered attractive, since the major portion of the invested capital can be generated in the form of a highly valued capitalized technology and specialized equipment. Other beneficial externalities and nontangible benefits aside, this can perhaps be considered as the most important lure for attracting business ventures to the selected European socialist countries.

## POSTSCRIPT

Studies dealing with the various aspects of joint ventures in socialist countries invariably open with the statement that this area represents a sudden

## TABLE 5.1

### Corporate Income Tax Rates of Western Countries

| Country | Statutory Tax Rate (Percent of Taxable Income) |
|---|---|
| Australia | 47.5 |
| Austria | 44.0 |
| Belgium | 33.0 |
| Canada | 50.0 |
| Denmark | 36.0 |
| Finland | 43.0 |
| France | 50.0 |
| Germany | 33.0* |
| Greece | 38.2 |
| Ireland | 50.0 |
| Italy | 43.8 |
| Japan | 31.4* |
| Luxembourg | 40.0 |
| Netherlands | 47.8 |
| Norway | 26.5 |
| Portugal | 21.8 |
| Spain | 32.8 |
| Sweden | 40.0 |
| Switzerland | 7.6 |
| Turkey | 25.0 |
| United Kingdom | 40.0 |
| United States | 48.0 |

*Average of tax rates on retained and distributed income.

*Source:* George Kopits, *International Comparison of Tax Depreciation Practises*, report prepared for the OECD Committee on Fiscal Affairs, Working Group no. 32 on Depreciation Practices, (Paris: OECD, August 1973).

new frontier for Western business firms in general and American enterprises in particular. Politicians, speaking in the same vein, urge capitalist entrepreneurs "to bring home the business." The present study proposes, however, that this "sudden new frontier" should be more critically examined and placed in a dynamic context.

Western as well as Soviet-bloc enterprises (Yugoslavia, due to her special case, is not part of this group) have been through the following similar stages of thought in regard to economic transactions with political adversaries:

*Cold war:* National security dominated and, therefore, one could not provide any tangible benefit to a political enemy that sought one's destruction. If this concept resulted in economic loss, it did not matter. Thus, the Western countries established embargoes, and Soviet-bloc states followed autarkic policies.

*Thaw:* If the assumed economic gains exceeded the estimated benefits of the adversary, then some limited economic transactions, subject to export controls, could be considered.

*Détente:* The most important goal was the relaxation of political tensions; therefore economic gains were secondary. It was hoped that the dynamics of this process would create externalities that would yield significant material benefits in the future. In this stage, Western firms experimented with token investments and, in the downward spiral of political tensions, a limited number of Soviet-bloc countries invited Western equity capital investments to demonstrate the end of confrontations and also to seek abolition of discriminatory tariffs, changes in export control policy, and other benefits.

*Normalcy:* Business firms, both Western and Soviet bloc, sought profits and profitability within the system under which they operated, and political considerations did not play a significant role.

In the present détente, both Western business establishments and Soviet bloc countries use strategies that, on purely economic grounds, could be considered unrealistic. It is to be expected that, when normalcy is achieved, these devices will be changed by a decision of a board of directors or by a new decree from a minister of finance. At present, Romania and Hungary are the only two Soviet-bloc countries that have opened up for joint business ventures with Western establishments. They offer various premiums to attract the attention of entrepreneurs, and they have a list of tax preferences, holidays, and outright exemptions. It is fair to suppose that these are only temporary. Their present aim is to assist the "trial investments" in order to lure additional ventures with more significant capital.

The practical implication of this proposition is that, if a long-run policy is considered, then Western investors should seek more stable concessions, such as depreciation-based deductions. This type of benefit is clear; it has a definite and known character. Since business contracts in these countries are still flexible, special concessions can be achieved by quid pro quo bargaining. One can trade some of the offered concessions, in the simplest case, for a depreciation rate that recovers the original costs. With problems of replacements, which are usually executed under rapidly changing prices, more complicated depreciation schemes should be proposed to meet the actual expenditures on replacements.

Will Western enterprise and its counterparts in different socialist countries achieve optimum production capacity in the stage of normalcy, when economic rationality dominates? In the case of market-socialist Yugoslavia, the prediction is an enthusiastic yes, especially if Yugoslavia devises a more rational and uniform tax scheme based on the so-called social contract among the various socialist republics and autonomous regions. Yugoslav enterprises

# CONCLUSIONS AND POSTSCRIPT

are granted complete freedom to determine the means and methods of management. Planning bodies make themselves felt only by influencing prices, taxes, and credit. Therefore, Yugoslavia is, in fact, a price-directed economy.

The same is not true, however, in the centrally planned systems of the Soviet bloc. To have the same structure as Yugoslavia, one must give up the most essential characteristics of a Soviet-type system: central planning. The much-heralded reforms have their strict limits; moreover, they are usually checked before they get very far. In Hungary the Central Committee of the party by its November 1972 decision indicated abatement in the application of flexibilities, and a trend toward reestablishment of a more regulated system is apparent. In Romania, the activity of enterprises is extremely limited, and transition to a more flexible system is not considered. It is, therefore, questionable that a joint business venture between a Western and Soviet-bloc firm will be able to function in the long run at the frontier of its production capacity, given the framework of a centrally planned economic system.

Some observers predict that Poland may experiment in the future with Western business ventures. However, one conclusion of the present study is that the Soviet Union and the Soviet-bloc countries of Bulgaria, Czechoslovakia, and the German Democratic Republic have realized the complexities and risks of the joint venture and are thus unlikely to engage in joint business undertakings on their own soil.

In view of all this, it may be asked whether some politicians, businessmen, and especially academicians have in fact overestimated the positive prospects for the joint equity-style business venture in Soviet-type countries. The proposition is that it is more rational and more realistic at this time to concentrate on the establishment of normal commercial relationships and various forms of business cooperation that do not require Western equity capital investments.

The change in atmospherics can be most successfully buttressed by concrete progress in these attainable and mutually desirable forms of economic cooperation. As for the tax policies of the selected socialist countries experimenting with joint ventures, the inescapable conclusion is that the regulations should be better coordinated with the investor's fiscal obligations in his own country. Without such harmonization, incentives can be meaningless and fiscal regulations may inhibit productive investment.

Finally the ticklish question of human rights and corporate responsibility can be raised. Various Western administrations, especially the government of the United States, are seeking to promote civil rights, political rights, and basic social and economic rights internationally. Is it opportune to give a helping hand to a repressive government that relies upon force for its authority, in exchange for profits? This question is neither treated nor answered in this study since it requires a separate investigation about the noneconomic costs and benefits of the investments of Western multinationals in communist countries in the present détente.

# APPENDIX
# A LIST OF
# YUGOSLAV STATUTES OF
# RELEVANCE TO FOREIGN INVESTMENT

## FUNDAMENTALS

The Constitution of the Socialist Federal Republic of Yugoslavia (*Official Gazette* of the SFRY no. 14/63)

The Amendments I to XLI to the Constitution of the Socialist Federal Republic of Yugoslavia (*Official Gazette* of the SFRY nos. 18/67, 55/68, and 29/71)

The Fundamental Law to Enforce the Constitutional Amendments XX to XLI (*Official Gazette* of the SFRY no. 29/71)

The Modified Fundamental Law to Enforce the Constitutional Amendments XX to XLI (*Official Gazette* of the SFRY no. 71/72)

The 1973 Draft Constitution of the Socialist Federal Republic of Yugoslavia

Resolution on the Basic Foundations of the Economic Policy in 1967 (*Official Gazette* of the SFRY no. 54/67)

Resolution on the Basic Foundations of the Economic Policy in 1969 (*Official Gazette* of the SFRY no. 51/68)

Resolution on the Basic Foundations of the Socio-economic Policy in 1970 (*Official Gazette* of the SFRY no. 56/69)

Resolution on the Basic Foundations of the Socio-economic Policy in 1971, with the Stabilization Program (*Official Gazette* of the SFRY no. 8/71)

Social Plan of Yugoslavia's Economic Development for the Period 1966–1970 (*Official Gazette* of the SFRY no. 28/66)

Social Plan of Yugoslavia's Economic Development for the Period 1971–1975 (*Official Gazette* of the SFRY no. 35/72)

Resolution on the Basic Foundations of the Policy of Yugoslavia's Socio-economic Development in 1973 (*Official Gazette* of the SFRY no. 71/72)

The Law Amending the Law on the Assets of Economic Organizations (*Official Gazette* of the SFRY nos. 31/67, 10/68, 24/68, 48/68, 42/69, 55/69, 28/70, and 34/71)

The Law on Trading Away the Social Assets Disposed of by the Basic Organizations of Associated Work (*Official Gazette* of the SFRY no. 22/73)

The Law on Foreign Investment into the Domestic Organizations of Associated Work (*Official Gazette* of the SFRY no. 22/73)

The Decree on Business Cooperation with Foreign Firms in the Free Customs Zones (*Official Gazette* of the SFRY no. 20/67)

## COMPANIES

The Basic Law on Enterprises (*Official Gazette* of the SFRY nos. 17/65, 31/67, 48/68, 55/69, and 15/71)

The Law on Establishment and Incorporation of the Organizations of Associated Work (*Official Gazette* of the SFRY no. 22/73)

The Law on the Title and the Name of the Organizations of Associated Work (*Official Gazette* of the SFRY no. 22/73)

The Basic Law on Simple Chambers of Economy and Business Cooperation in the Economy (*Official Gazette* of the SFRY nos. 28/60, 16/61, 13/63, 10/65, 31/67, and 51/68)

The Law on Operational Combining (*Official Gazette* of the SFRY no. 23/72)

The Directives Concerning Opening and Cancelling Drawing and Other Accounts of the Beneficiaries of the Social Assets with the Social Accountancy Board (*Official Gazette* of the SFRY no. 58/73)

## FOREIGN TRADE

The Law on Turnover of Goods and Services as Amended (*Official Gazette* of the SFRY no. 26/72)

## CUSTOMS DUTY

The Customs Duty Law (*Official Gazette* of the SFRY no. 22/73)

The Law on Customs Tariff (*Official Gazette* of the SFRY nos. 34/65, 49/66, 5/67, 54/67, 9/68, 22/68, 30/68, 17/69, 27/69, 52/69, 22/70, 25/70, 58/71, 63/72, and 71/72)

The Decision on Duty Free Importation of Certain Equipment That Is Temporarily Brought in to a Free Customs Zone (*Official Gazette* of the SFRY no. 20/67)

The Decree Defining Conditions for Temporary Importation of Goods (*Official Gazette* of the SFRY no. 42/73)

## FOREIGN EXCHANGE

The Law on Foreign Exchange Transactions (*Official Gazette* of the SFRY nos. 36/72 and 71/72)

## TAXATION

The Law on Profit Tax Payable by Foreign Persons Investing in a Domestic Economic Organization for Running Business in Common (*Official Gazette* of the SFRY nos. 31/67 and 9/68)

The Law on Profit Tax Concessions Favoring Foreign Persons Investing in a Domestic Organization for Running Business in Common (*Official Gazette* of the S.R. of Montenegro no. 23/69)

The Law on Profit Tax Concessions Favoring Foreign Persons Investing in a Domestic Organization for Running Business in Common (*Official Gazette* of the S.R. of Macedonia no. 42/71)

The Law Supplementing the Law on the Establishment of Interest Rates on the Funds in the Economy (*Official Gazette* of the SFRY no. 31/67)

The Law Supplementing the Basic Law on the Contributions and Taxes Payable by Citizens (*Official Gazette* of the SFRY no. 31/67)

The Decision Concerning Special Contributions, Income, Auditing and Profit Taxes Payable by the Foreign Contractors of Investments Works in Yugoslavia (*Official Gazette* of the SFRY no. 15/67)

A Law on Income Tax of the Organizations of Associated Work (*Official Monitor* of the S.R. of Serbia no. 4/73)

## INCOME

The Law on the Establishment and Computation of Total Receipts and Income in the Basic Organizations of Associated Work (*Official Gazette* of the SFRY no. 71/72)

## BOOKKEEPING AND AUDITING

The Law on the Bookkeeping in the Work Organizations (*Official Gazette* of the SFRY nos. 48/68 and 56/69)

The Law on the Revaluation of the Assets of the Organizations of Associated Work (*Official Gazette* of the SFRY no. 50/71)

Directive on How to Materialize Revaluation of the Assets of the Organizations of Associated Work and to Report for the Sake of Social Records (*Official Gazette* of the SFRY no. 51/71)

## LABOR

The Law on Mutual Relations of Workers in the Associated Work (*Official Gazette* of the SFRY no. 22/73)

Regulations on Particular Conditions for Hiring Foreign Citizens by a Work Organization (*Official Gazette* of the SFRY no. 43/65)

The Law on Confining the Construction of an Investment Facility to a Foreign Contractor (*Official Gazette* of the SFRY nos. 53/70 and 40/73)

## MISCELLANEOUS

Decree on Conditions for the Operation of the Foreign Firms' Representations in Yugoslavia (*Official Gazette* of the SFRY nos. 38/68, 22/69, and 10/71)

Decree on Long-Term Production Cooperation Between Domestic Organizations of Associated Work and Foreign Persons (*Official Gazette* of the SFRY no. 7/73)

# BIBLIOGRAPHY

## BOOKS

Ady, P. (ed.), *Private Foreign Investment and the Developing World*, (New York: Praeger, 1971).

Bergsten, F., Moran, T., and Horst, T., *American Multinationals and American Interests*, (Washington, D.C.: Brookings Institute, 1976).

Brooke, M. Z., and Remmers, H. L., *The Multinational Company in Europe*, (London: Longmans, 1972).

Friedman, W. G., and Mates L. (eds.), *Joint Business Ventures of Yugoslav Enterprises and Foreign Firms*, (New York: Rothman, 1968).

Friedman, W. G., and Beguib, J. P., *Joint International Business Ventures in Developing Countries: Case Studies and Analysis of Recent Trends*, (New York: Columbia University Press, 1971).

Hufbauer, G. S., et al., *U. S. Taxation of American Business Abroad: An Exchange of Views*, (Washington, D. C.: American Enterprise for Public Policy Research, 1972).

Kenen, P., *International Trade and Finance: Frontier for Research*, (Cambridge: Cambridge University Press, 1975).

Kretchmar, R. S., and Foor, R., *The Potential for Joint Ventures in Eastern Europe*, (New York: Praeger, 1972).

Marer, P., *Soviet and East European Foreign Trade, 1946–1969*, (Bloomington: Indiana University Press, 1972).

Marer, P., *Hungary's Industrial Cooperation with the West: Achievements, Problems and Perspectives*, mimeo. (October 1975), prepared for the U. S. Chamber of Commerce.

McMillan, C. H., and St. Charles, D. P., *Joint Ventures in Eastern Europe: A Three-Country Comparison*, (Ottawa: The Canadian Economic Policy Committee, C. D. Howe Research Institute, 1973).

Musgrave, P. B., *United States Taxation of Foreign Investment Income: Issues and Arguments*, (Cambridge: Harvard Law School International Tax Program, 1969).

Musgrave, R. A., *Fiscal Systems*, (New Haven: Yale University Press, 1969).

## ARTICLES

Adler, G., and Hufbauer, G. C., "Foreign Investment Controls; Objective-Removal," *Columbia Journal and World Business* (May-June 1969).

Fleck, F. H., and Mantouz, R., "The Multinational Corporation: Tax Avoidance and Profit Manipulation via Subsidiaries and Tax Havens," *Schweizerishe Zeitschrift fur Volksvirtschaft and Statistik* (June 1974).

Hewett, E. D., "The Economics of East European Technology Imports from the West," *American Economic Review* (May 1975).

Holt, J. B., "The Rules for Western Multinationals in Eastern Europe," *Columbia Journal of World Business* (Fall 1973).

Horst, T., "The Theory of the Multinational Firm: Optimal Behavior under Different Tariff and Tax Rates," *Journal of Political Economy* (April-May 1971).

Horst, T., "The Simple Analytics of Multi-National Firm Behavior," in *International Trade and Money*, edited by B. Connolly and A. K. Swoboda, (London: George Allen & Unwin, 1973).

Hufbauer, G. C., "Multinational Corporations and the International Adjustment Process," *American Economic Review, Papers and Proceedings* (May 1974).

Jonas, P., "The Redistribution of the Product-Mix in a Centrally Planned Economy," *Southern Economic Journal* (July 1968).

Jonas, P., "Unilateral Transfers in a Soviet-Type Economy," *Indian Economic Journal* (January-March 1971).

Nagy, T., "Hungary: Taxation of Foreign Companies, Economic Associations with Foreign Participation and Foreign Nationals," *Interta: European Law Review* (June 1975).

Sukijasović, M., "Foreign Investment in Yugsolavia," in *Foreign Investment: The Experience in Host Countries*, edited by I. A. Litvak and C. J. Maule, (New York: Praeger, 1970).

## GOVERNMENTAL AND INTERGOVERNMENTAL PUBLICATIONS

Jonas, P., *Taxation of Western Enterprise in Selected European Socialist Countries*, (Washington, D. C.: Office of Tax Analysis, U. S. Department of Treasury, OTA Paper 13, May 1976).

U. N. Department of Economics and Social Affairs, *Multinational Corporations in World Development*, (New York: United Nations, 1972; Document No. ST/ECA/190).

U. S. Department of Commerce, *The Multinational Corporation, Studies on U. S. Foreign Investment*, in two volumes, (Washington, D. C.: Volume 1, 1972; Volume 11, 1973).

U. S. Department of State, "Report on the Convention Between the United States and the Socialist Republic of Romania, Signed December 4, 1973," (Washington, D. C.: Commerce Clearing House) (Tax Treaties, 7351 A).

U. S. Congress, Senate Committee on Foreign Relations, *Tax Conventions with Poland, Iceland, and Romania*—Report to Accompany Executives A, E, and B. Exec. Rep. No. 94-15, 94th Congress, 1st sess. (Washington, D. C.: USGPO, 1975).

## BIBLIOGRAPHIES

Aronson, J. D., *The Multinational Corporation, The Nation, State and the International System: A Bibliography,* mimeo. (Stanford; Stanford University Department of Political Science, June, 1973).

Lall, S., *Foreign Private Manufacturing Investment and Multinational Corporations: An Annotated Bibliography,* (New York: Praeger, 1975).

Owens, E., and Hovenmeyer, G., *Bibliography on Taxation of Foreign Operations and Foreigners 1968-1975,* (Cambridge, Mass.: International Tax Program, The Law School of Harvard University, 1976).

U. N. Secretariat, *Multinational Corporations: A Select Bibliography,* (New York: United Nations, Document No. ST/LIB/30, August 1973).

## SERIES

*Bulletin for International Fiscal Documentation,* (Amsterdam: International Bureau of Fiscal Documentation).

*Journal of Taxation,* (New York: Journal of Taxation, Inc.).

*World Tax Series,* (Cambridge: Harvard University, Harvard Law School International Program in Taxation).

## COMPUTER FACILITIES

*Soviet and East European Trade Data Bank,* International Development Research Center, Indiana University, 1005 East Tenth Street, Bloomington, Indiana.

## ABOUT THE AUTHOR

PAUL JONAS is Professor of Economics at the University of New Mexico. Until 1968 he was Associate Professor of Economics at Brooklyn College of the City University of New York. His first teaching assignment was at the School of Commerce and Finance, New York University.

Dr. Jonas has published widely in the areas of economic growth, planning, and comparative systems. His monographs have been published by the U.S. Agency for International Development and the Department of Treasury and include *Projections and Forecasts for the Indian Economy 1969–1980,* volumes 1–3, and *Taxation of Western Enterprise in Selected Socialist Countries.* His articles and reviews have appeared in, among other professional publications, the *Journal of Political Economy, Review of Economics and Statistics, Oxford Economic Papers, American Economic Review, Econometrica, Southern Economic Journal, Annals of Regional Science, Indian Economic Journal, Pakistan Development Review,* and *Jahrbuch der Wirtschaft Osteouropas.* An autobiographical article was published in *Harper's.*

Dr. Jonas holds a diploma and doctorate of Economics from the University of Technical and Economic Sciences, Budapest, Hungary. After arriving in the United States in 1957, he received additional training at Yale and Columbia Universities and has a Ph.D. in economics from Columbia.

Dr. Jonas served as an economic-statistical advisor to the U.S. Agency for International Development India Mission, New Delhi and spent a sabbatical year as a Senior Fulbright-Hays Scholar at the University of Islamabad, Pakistan.

**RELATED TITLES**
Published by
Praeger Special Studies


THE MULTINATIONAL BUSINESSMAN AND FOREIGN POLICY:
Entreprenurial Politics in East-West Trade and Investment
　　　　　　　　　Jeffrey M. Brookstone

THE POLITICAL ECONOMY OF EAST-WEST TRADE
　　　　　　　　　Connie M. Friesen

FINANCING FOREIGN TRADE IN EASTERN EUROPE:
Problems of Bilateralism and Currency Inconvertibility
　　　　　　　　　John S. Garland

TECHNOLOGY TRANSFER TO EAST EUROPE:
U. S. Corporate Experience
　　　　　　　　　Eric W. Hayden

TECHNOLOGY TRANSFER AND U.S. FOREIGN POLICY
　　　　　　　　　Henry R. Nau